TO DIE FOR

TO DIE FOR

100 gastronomic experiences to have before you die

STEPHEN DOWNES

PIER 9

Contents

Introduction

Strictly speaking, I suppose, *To Die For* should be retitled *To Die After*. It contains what I believe to be the world's essential eating experiences—the best. And, while you have a life, you ought to try to fit my suggestions into it. Obviously, someone in the developing world who has neither the opportunity nor the money to eat for pleasure must miss out on many of my top one hundred. (Yet several of the experiences I list are enjoyed on a daily basis by people of very meagre means.) However, those of us in rich countries—even people of middling incomes—have no excuse, in my view, for declining to appreciate the widest possible range of good food prepared from raw ingredients.

And that's really what the best eating experiences almost always are. Simple food prepared by hand from great basic makings. It's what this book is all about, at any rate. Indeed, while you need to go to restaurants to experience many of the dishes I write about, the majority can be prepared at home. I've assembled them under four headings: 'Eating out', 'Eating in', 'Worth the effort', and 'Perfect 10s'. They range from enjoying one of the world's most baroque pieces of culinary architecture, Tim Pak Poy's snow eggs, to gorging on a ripe mango. Many vegetarian delights are included.

My subconscious no doubt considered thousands of eating experiences before I decided on my top one hundred. Those in this book must, of course, be mine—the list is totally subjective and you don't need to protest that it excludes many countless acts of magnificent mastication. But, on purpose, my list has tried to summarize the highlights of my gustatory life on the world's major continents. It is drawn from almost three decades as a professional palate.

What *To Die For* is *not* is easy to say. It's not a collection of recipes. You will see few precise quantities of ingredients in this book. I'm more interested in how cooks conceive their dishes, what they were attempting to do with the four basic flavours (salt, sour, sweet and bitter) and the textures they employed. You cannot begin to cook if you don't understand these basics, in my opinion. I believe you can learn a lot about preparing perfect food from a book like mine, where what you are trying to achieve and how you go about getting there are uppermost. You have to know what you're trying to do when you cook—the tastes and textures and balances you are attempting to create. You have to be able to tell when food is excellent or, on the other hand, not worth your juices. Too few of us can.

My book is not simply a checklist, either, an exercise in boasting about the expensive top-restaurant offerings I have engulfed. It has a didactic core. Simply stated, *To Die For* contains most of what I know about the principles of cooking and eating. I see it as a primer on taste both in the physiological and philosophical sense. I hope it tells readers how to eat.

I never notice the time I spend cooking because it's such a joy. An afternoon might pass, and, deep in concentration, I'm unaware of the ebbing hours. Why? Because I'm watching miraculous mutations of substances to produce something extraordinarily appetizing—perfect. I love cooking for that reason; it's the only thing I can sometimes do perfectly. The dish in front of you, something you have created from scratch, cannot be improved on, you say to yourself. And it's so often true! What a reward! It leaves me trembling with excitement every time I achieve it. I am literally breathless. And if I chose not to spend a couple of hours producing this peerless tucker? Well, I might prepare a poor meal instead, watch execrable television, read an airport novel or listen to wallpaper music. The food manufacturers gull us constantly into believing that the time they save us is invaluable. Yet most of us don't value time at all. We waste it. What profound returns we would get instead by using time for cooking! (It's also better for our health.)

I am only too aware, though, that *To Die For* is written partly in protest at the comprehensive victory of poor food over good, the annihilation of proper cooking in many homes by food processed for huge material gain by big corporations. Food developed with artificial flavours and colours is an abomination and we must never cease from saying it. Apart from its inferiority, it is also killing us—killing our souls, our imaginations and our differences. (And possibly our bodies as well.) So *To Die For* aims to encourage your return to natural cooking. It gives you a clear route towards that goal and ways of determining if you are on course.

My list begins. Tick off my selections as you experience them. I hope, though, that *To Die For* will spur you to cook more often at home, to appreciate great food a little bit more, to revel in a fresh apple rather than tearing open a packet of chips.

Eating out

Four dances of the sea

When Cheong Liew closed his famed restaurant Neddy's after almost thirteen years, he wrote a valedictory menu, subtitling it 'The dance is over'. (Among its items was a salad of crocodile tail and aubergine.) It was 1988, and few people in hospitality expected to see Cheong back behind the burners. Ever again. After all, he was joining Regency Hotel School to teach—a far less frenetic business. He had yearned for financial stability—he and his wife Mary's fourth child had arrived—and he admits himself that he was 'in a rut' at Neddy's.

But Cheong Liew is one of the indisputable fathers of Australian cooking, and perhaps you just can't keep a good chef down. After all, he had taught the South Australian capital how to eat, and dishes such as exotic cartilage in a carrot–chilli sauce were commonplace at Neddy's by the late 1970s. Not bad for a man who had taught himself to cook by reading books.

Cheong had had an interesting life. Born in Kuala Lumpur in 1949, he was the son of a chicken farmer. He remembers picking the tiny feathers from swiftlets' nests that would be soaked to create the famous soup. After anti-Chinese riots in 1969, his family fled Malaysia, a Chinese diaspora that resulted in Cheong coming first to Melbourne then joining his brother in Adelaide. Unable to succeed as a student of electronic engineering, he began short-order cooking—fried rice and pub snacks. He cooked in a Greek restaurant and a steak restaurant. And all the while he read about the culinary arts from the best sources. Soon, cooking was his passion.

Among many others, the legendary French chef Paul Bocuse has said that cooking is about what's in the fridge. In Adelaide in the 1970s, cooking for Cheong was about what he could buy fresh at the market. Inevitably, compromises with ingredients had to be made, and he found himself blending European techniques and 'Asian' ingredients. And thence to Neddy's, and a certain esteem for this strange new fusion food, which he was producing, we need to remember, long before anyone in California or Europe had even storyboarded a pitch on East–West cuisine. (The 'fusion' idea simply became a marketing tool a little later.)

And then he closed Neddy's doors and took up a whiteboard marker at Regency. In the early 1990s, you'd go to Adelaide and hear that Cheong was doing a guest stint at some obscure pub's brasserie. You'd chase down the place to discover his short 'season' had ended. There was a palpable feeling around town that Adelaide wanted Cheong Liew back. The city's gastronomes— pound for pound, Adelaide has more of them than any other Australian capital—were missing him.

Eventually, executives at the Adelaide Hilton had the perspicacity and persistence to entice him to return to a commercial kitchen. With Cheong in charge, the Hilton wanted to relaunch its premium restaurant, The Grange, under the slogan 'Let the dance begin'. And over six hours and even more cigarettes (he used to roll his own but has now given up smoking) one night in the mid-1990s, Cheong created a signature dish for his—and the restaurant's— rebirth. In my view, it should be declared Australia's national dish. It has the characteristic elements of our national cooking style; a variety of ingredients and appropriate techniques are used, irrespective of their origins. And Cheong called the dish 'four dances of the sea'.

It amounted to four small islands of seafood on a bare white plate. There were tiny fillets of soused snook (a kind of pike) on avocado slices with a wasabi mayonnaise, slivers of raw cuttlefish with squid-ink noodles, slices of poached octopus tentacles with a garlic mayonnaise, and spicy prawn sushi with glutinous rice. They were arranged at the points of the compass, and eaten in the order in which I've listed them, which meant you ascended in strength of flavour. Each mouthful had meaning. The snook, for instance, was dedicated to a Japanese friend who came to Regency to teach students how to pickle fish. The octopus was there to remember The Iliad, the Greek restaurant where Cheong had discovered the joy of cooking. And the prawn was a salute to his childhood in Malaysia.

Riots would break out if The Grange took four dances off its list. It's built from about fifty separate ingredients and all Australians should eat it at least once. Especially politicians, who need to be continually reminded that two of Australia's best chefs were refugees. And that our national dish is not pie 'n' sauce or steak and chips. We don't need to cringe. We lead the world, but our leaders neither know nor care.

Whole red snapper barbecued over coconut husks

Jimbaran Bay in Bali is a wide arc of fine sandy beach facing due west. Its waters are relatively calm most of the time, and at dusk they are glassy, producing that mirrored gunmetal sheen that you can smell as well as see in Joseph Conrad's novels. You'd never know it, but obscured in the strip of tropical vegetation behind the sand are a couple of luxury hotels. And over the past dozen years or so, scores of open-air cafés have sprouted along the beach as well.

You get to them either by walking along the sand or taking a taxi to a narrow service road running behind it. Two prominent strings of cafés are at the north end of the beach near the fishing village that provides the catch. A third group is at the southern end. I've tried several over the years and can recommend Jimbaran Beach Café. In all of them the format is similar. Seafood is on display in ice slurries in big polystyrene boxes near the service road. You choose what you want to eat and pay by weight. The selection varies according to the season and the weather, of course, but there are usually plenty of silver and red snapper, calamari, big sea prawns (not farmed ones) and large heavy-shelled clams.

Then you're taken down to the sand where your table awaits. Most people want to face the water and watch the sun go down. If you arrive early enough you should get a front-row seat. The chairs are plastic, as is the floral tablecloth. Meanwhile, on the other side of the service road in open-fronted shacks your seafood is being slung on the barbie. Some barbie! They're halves of forty-four-gallon drums containing red-hot coconut husks, a wire grill over the top. You're welcome to watch as each café's special sauce—usually a red oily concoction containing garlic, chilli and tamarind juice—is liberally brushed over the seafood as it grills.

The results, of course, are sublime. And extras are thrown in for the price of the seafood. At Jimbaran Beach Café these included boiled potatoes; swamp cabbage wok-tossed with chilli and soy; a tomato, cucumber and shallot salad; steamed rice and several sauces, among them a sweet garlic–soy juice, chilli–lemon grass and chilli–garlic. The sun sets; a waist-deep fisherman hurls his *filet*, which hangs in the pale air for an eternity before plopping on the glassy water, and the lights of Java begin to twinkle on the horizon.

The snapper can't be beaten, the clams arrive in their shells in a wonderful sweet-soy paste and items such as calamari and prawns are so fresh they fight you before being swallowed. In 2002 a meal for two with two large bottles of beer cost on average about $26. Stuffed.

Janni's tripe

Janni Kyritsis came to Australia from Greece as an electrician and became one of our best cooks. In particular, the tripe he cooked at Berowra Waters Inn then Bennelong and MG Garage was sublime. I ate it every time I could. Indeed, I eat tripe whenever I see it listed. So should you.

Forget the absolutely disgusting—I completely agree with you, you see—Anglo–Celtic tripe in white sauce with chopped parsley some of our mothers used to make. Its major problem was that nothing foiled the flesh—it was not only in your mouth but also in your face. The slugs of stomach lining simply sulked in a flour–milk–butter miasma of matching colour.

Janni's tripe, indeed, most restaurant tripe dishes these days, will have rich, sweet vegetable flavours. The best restaurants in which to search for them are usually of Italian persuasion.

The interesting thing about Janni's tripe was its name and origin—'lyonnaise tripe'. If I searched standard reference books, Janni once told me, I'd be unlikely to find a tripe dish named after the great French gastronomic capital, Lyon. He and Tony Bilson had created it for Berowra Waters Inn, he said. From the Inn's earliest days in the mid-1970s, Tony had listed it on the menu. Janni, who was chef there a decade later after Tony had split from partner Gay, turned it into a classic. So it was a joint effort, Janni conceded.

Now, to understand that sentence you will need to know that a main theme running through Tony Bilson's culinary career is what he calls *à la minute* cooking. Cooking to order, you might call it in English. His lyonnaise tripe was a matter of frying tripe and onions then adding a demi-glace (*see* 'A great brown sauce') and tomato sauce. A dash of vinegar and sprinkle of parsley completed it. Very systematic at the stove, Janni couldn't work that way. It was 'too hit and miss', he told me. So, instead, he perfected a longish stew of tripe and aromatic vegetables. The result was to cry for, this gluey, green, sweet and tomato-strong ragout.

For all Janni's contentions about the absence of tripe 'lyonnaise' from recipe books, I couldn't help checking. Escoffier, Larousse and Margaret Fulton all had a lyonnaise tripe, two calling it 'tripe and onions'. They agreed that it was fried tripe to which separately fried chopped onions were added. Heated vinegar (or lemon juice, in Margaret's case) was poured over just before serving and parsley sprinkled. So Tony Bilson was right. Give tripe a go at home, too. Ask your butcher if his is ready for stewing, and you should leave it simmering for at least ninety minutes.

Salmon with sorrel

Frankly, it surprises me that this most emblematic dish of nouvelle cuisine has been so little copied. To taste it in its native territory you're going to have to journey all the way to Roanne, a modest town near the mighty Rhone River in south-eastern France. More specifically, you will have to eat it at the esteemed restaurant Troisgros, where the dish was created. But, lucky you, Troisgros' salmon with sorrel is so famous it's always available. I've seen it made, and what strikes you most is its simplicity. In my view, it has succeeded so hugely as a piece of culinary art because the sweetness and slightly cloying texture of salmon foils the high acidity and extremely narrow flavour range of the sorrel leaves, which are 'melted' into a sauce.

Sorrel leaves are spear-shaped. Wild sorrel, a small, low-growing plant, sprouts in suburban gardens at least in southern Australia and may be eaten. Indeed, I once had a marvellous home-cooked soup that used it with mussels. Cultivated sorrel has much bigger leaves. Both sorts, though, contain oxalic acid, which is also in rhubarb and its leaves, and provides a high, but not at all unpleasant, sharpness.

Thirty years ago I tasted the Troisgros brothers' salmon with sorrel for the first time. I was overwhelmed by it then, and it would astound me as much today. It was the salmon dish to end them all. Pierre Troisgros once told me—in the middle of a conversation about Australian football, funnily enough—that he wished he had a dollar for every dish of salmon with sorrel he'd sold. Of course, he'd be lessening his return; the Troisgros brothers made very much more than a dollar a dish from their salmon–sorrel, I suspect, even in the very earliest days of its existence.

Pierre and Jean Troisgros grew up in Roanne's Hôtel des Platanes, which was owned by their parents. They trained as chefs at Lucas-Carton in Paris then with the great, king-making Fernand Point at the esteemed La Pyramide at Vienne. Returning home to the Platanes in the 1960s, they renamed its restaurant Les Frères Troisgros and first scored Michelin's highest award, three *macarons* (stars for us) in 1968. (Jean died in 1983 and these days the restaurant is simply called Troisgros.)

Pierre told me that they began cooking their salmon with sorrel in the mid-1960s, even before the first murmurings of discontent that led to the nouvelle cuisine breakaway by top French chefs and its quasi-official launching in the October 1973 edition of *Le Nouveau Guide Gault-Millau*. It is an artless concoction, but you should try to cook it at home.

Skinned and boned salmon fillets are gently flattened between sheets of greaseproof paper. Fish stock, dry white wine, white Vermouth and finely chopped shallots are reduced in a pan to a glistening syrup. Cream is added and the sauce is boiled and thickened again. Washed, dried and destalked sorrel leaves go in next and, after less than half a minute, the sauce is taken off the heat and finished with butter, a few drops of lemon juice and seasoning. The salmon fillets are fried 'dry' in a non-stick pan for twenty-five seconds on their first side and fifteen on the second. (Mind you, there are no timers in the Troisgros kitchen. This kind of thing is all about touch and whether you've got it.)

Sauce goes on the plate first, then the fish, best side up. And the result is exquisite, a perfect example of the blending of basic flavours—saltiness, sourness, sweetness (from the fish and vermouth) and bitterness (from the sorrel).

Murray cod at Stefano's

I'm citing a restaurant—Stefano's in Mildura's Grand Hotel—in which to eat your Murray cod, but, in truth, it can't be done. Certainly, chef Stefano de Pieri can procure farmed versions of this iconic and fabulous fish. But in the old days, before recent legislation prevented it, he was able to buy big native fish straight from anglers. And he and his kitchen team did a fabulous job cooking them.

I'm quoting Stefano because he knew what to do with such gelatinous and subtly tasting flesh. (And if you haven't tasted real, wild Murray cod cooked well then you simply must. Don't die without doing it—you will never forgive yourself.) Halfway through a conversation with Stefano on this very subject, he upbraided a third party who had overheard us for grilling it. It was too delicate for that, he insisted, too easily turned to a desiccated parody of the fresh product.

Indeed, when Murray cod were occasionally seen in shops and markets, most older Australians knew how to ruin it. Some didn't, of course. A bloke who painted our suburban Melbourne home from time to time when I was a child used to put down his brushes to gaze wistfully into the middle distance whenever he talked Murray cod. It was the best-eating fish in the world, he murmured. He spent his entire holidays camped by the Murray catching this 'genius' of a fish, as he called it. And his wife knew how to cook it. He brought cod sandwiches from home one day, tore off a corner of flesh from a thick steak and gave it to me. I understood what he was getting at. On another occasion, he dropped in fresh steaks—cross-sections of a very big fish—for my mother to fry. Despite her general lack of interest in fancy cooking, she produced a memorable meal. (I think the fish did much of the work.) So let's hope new conservation regulations work, the Murray runs full again, the carp die off and the cod fingerlings released each year prosper.

In Stefano's, a brick-lined cellar restaurant that you should try even if Murray cod is unlisted, I've eaten the real thing perhaps three times. It was always simply and quickly done, says Stefano. He would use fillets from big to very big fish. Portions were dusted with—'rolled in', as he put it—plain flour and lightly fried in butter and oil containing pancetta pieces and sage for half a minute each side. Cooking continued in the oven, where the cod cuts would be baked for five to six minutes in a moderate oven. Curiously, the sauce he served with them was usually based on a classic lamb reduction, perhaps beginning with a stock made from neck and aromatic vegetables. He didn't mention it, but I would be surprised if the pancetta and sage from the frying didn't join the lamb reduction at some stage. At any rate, the cod was plated with the lamb sauce, and the whole point of the dish was 'to tease ourselves and you', said Stefano. It was a kind of freshwater version of surf and turf, he laughed.

Broad beans and artichokes

When I grew up, you were aware of iodine in only one form: an ointment that went on bruises. It was black and thick. And if you were bruised badly enough and needed several applications, you couldn't wash off the stuff for weeks. Moreover, you stank of it. Nowadays, of course, we happily eat iodine flavours in one of the most exalted of all vegetables, the humble artichoke, a derivative of the thistle.

Like other arts, cooking is about blending affinities or contrasting differences. An absolutely brilliant dish I discovered blends two vegetables of very close tastes and, especially, textures. Think of broad beans and artichokes. Their seeds unpeeled, the beans have a fine feltiness—as do hearts of artichokes. Both have a light bitterness. And in the case of artichoke, there are distinct tones of iodine as well as the strong mineral flavours common also in the beans. How or why would you partner such similarities in the one dish?

I can't answer that question, but I do know that Piraeus Blues, a Greek restaurant in Melbourne that specializes in traditional home cooking, does it brilliantly. You must make every effort to try their kingly double-vegetable stew. First, it's something of a cooking miracle; both the beans and halves of small artichokes come out perfectly cooked, their forms intact yet seductively soft and smeary, their chlorophyll, mineral and iodine flavours strong, comforting and full. The dish uses quite a length of the artichokes' stalks and trims them only a little. Then both artichoke halves and beans are fried with crushed garlic and onions in olive oil. Water and seasoning is added; a lid goes on top and the lot is simmered until tender. To thicken the juice, flour stirred into cold water is added. Choppings of fresh dill and a spray or two of lemon juice are added just before tabling.

I have tried several times to replicate this brilliant concoction, by the way, and failed miserably, never getting even close to its robust delights. I shouldn't wonder why. Dishes like these and the secret sleights of hand by which they succeed are worked out over centuries in places such as Greek villages. The result is a kind of artless simplicity we these days take for granted. It's no coincidence that two elderly Greek women who are related to the owners actually cook the dish. Nor should we forget that the ancient Greeks—and Romans—were the first to harvest thistles. They've had a long time to get the recipe right.

Thousand-year-old eggs

Are you ready for an unnerving trip? Because we're about to head into a gastronomic heart of darkness. Up a gustatory river few gourmets have cruised. We are about to taste thousand-year-old eggs, that great Cantonese delicacy. It's dare territory I'm leading you into; a dubious region where there is no respite from deep-fried insects, snake soups and poached embryos, no outpost of progress, no Mr Kurtz—neither alive nor dead—to take us in and offer us ambiguity or the succour of safe and stodgy European tucker.

Known as 'pei daan' in Hong Kong, thousand-year-old eggs aren't anywhere near that old—they've been around only a little over a month. And before you break into them you must crack open their sandy-coloured coating of clay and rice husks. (Another form of Chinese preserved egg is coated with ash.) Once inside, your egg sliced in half, the sight will both repel and fascinate you. The yolks of these delicacies are the colour and consistency of axle grease. Faint green concentric rings circle their edges. And beyond the yolk, what used to be the protein-rich white has become transparent, the consistency of hard jelly and the colour of best-quality amber. In the mouth, the textures alone will make you want either to vomit or expectorate. Champion eaters, men and women of gustatory courage, those who know that you masticate only when you see the whites of their eggs, will chew on, to be met by a strangely palatable but execrable taste that I can best describe as rotting vegetables flavoured with fresh herbs.

It all makes sense when you realize that thousand-year-old eggs are created by burial in a marinade of salt, wheat and 'mud', as an expert put it to me. (I suspect that the mud is somewhat special.) What happens to the egginess of the egg remains a mystery.

And just why anyone would create a taste delight of such ambivalence is beyond my understanding. You eat them raw, and rather than take the risk of trying thousand-year-old eggs when and where you see them, let me recommend those of the wonderful Yung Kee restaurant in Hong Kong's Central district. A veteran place heading into its seventh decade, Yung Kee serves them at the start of the meal with large slices of pink, house-pickled ginger. They're big eggs, too, usually from ducks.

Chinese traditionally chop thousand-year-old eggs into their morning congee (a kind of rice porridge) or add them to steamed custard. Heroes eat them raw—as we did, of course.

Breakfast at the Hotel Saigon Morin

Big hotels make kings' ransoms selling breakfast. I remember a hospitality executive once telling me that rustling up the first meal of the day for business types and travellers was virtually a licence to print cash. (Or credit cards, as is the case these days.) Charges for buffet breakfasts were especially loaded, reflecting up to six times the cost to the hotel of preparing and serving the food.

So you can tell a lot about a place's attitude to its guests, I believe, from what it serves them for breakfast. And the best hotel breakfast I can remember eating—and it's fairly recent, too—was at the Hotel Saigon Morin in Hue, the old Vietnamese imperial capital.

The Morin has not rewarded me in even the slightest of ways to write the following words, and I booked and paid what was duly demanded—as anyone else would—via the Internet. But if I was about to have my lights extinguished and had a night and a breakfast left, it would be extremely difficult to dissuade me from taking them in the Morin. First of all, it's a hotel of the greatest South-East-Asian, tea-party-type charm—the kind of place Raffles used to be before profiteering took over. It turned one hundred in 2001 and was renovated to its former glory only a few years before. In this small provincial city, it dominates a central intersection, its four-storeyed whitewashed wings extending what seems a hundred metres or more down perpendicular streets. The rooms are huge, luxurious and very economically priced. They have decorative cast-iron balconies overlooking the street, ceramic artefacts on display, fruit baskets and comfortable armchairs. In the Morin's long wide corridors hang an archive of black-and-white photographs that tell the hotel's history—and, incidentally, much of Hue's, too.

The Hotel Saigon Morin is the kind of place where the ancient art of turning down your bed has been resurrected. And at retirement, you'll also find pillowside a gluey, sesame-covered sweet and a philosophical story on fancy paper tied up with scarlet ribbon. The hotel is built around quite spacious gardens, including a kind of palm court. It needs a great all-weather bar, and the appalling muzak that fills its corridors should be annihilated. Then it would be perfect.

You can't really fault its breakfast buffet, at least for food quality and choice. (The coffee must come from machines but is pretty good.) From day to day the offerings change, too, so that the same range of eats is never displayed on successive days. I took a pen to one of my three breakfasts at the Morin and noted that there were eight sorts of cakes, many of them containing a pastry cream or custard of some sort. (Two days before there had been light cooked crèmes in Chinese ceramic spoons flecked with vanilla 'dust'.) Then there were nine sorts of breads, and I haven't included excellent croissants among the cakes. There were boiled eggs, poached eggs, fried eggs, thousand-year-old eggs (see 'Thousand-year-old eggs') and made-to-order omelettes. (You chose from a host of ingredients, among them cheese, fresh tomato choppings, baby mushrooms, ham, onion, chilli, mint and bean shoots.) There was congee (rice porridge) and caramelized prawns in a kind of sweet thick sauce. There were preserved vegetables such as Korean-style pickled cabbage. Hash potatoes, tasty small frankfurters and crisp bacon were kept hot over spirit burners. There were cold meats and a tomato and cucumber salad. Cold crepes and cereals made an appearance.

Then there were wonderful house-made jams clearly put together from only fruit and sugar (see 'My plum jam'). One was a marmalade—Vietnam grows terrific citrus fruit—another apple, a third mainly pineapple if I was not mistaken, and a fourth strawberry. And toasters to toast your bread in. Six sorts of fresh fruit, many cut into bite-sized peeled morsels, were for the taking. Pho was next (see 'Pho')—the terrific Hue version, called 'bun bo', of the great soup of Vietnam. Thin slices of raw beef are simmered for about half a minute in a large ladle of stock then poured over rice noodles, slices of cooked beef, spring onions and other ingredients to produce what some experts believe is the world's mother-broth.

I'm sure I've probably left out several things, but you're still confronting heaven in a breakfast.

Fruit-bat stew

I felt more like a palaeontologist than a professional gourmet. Here I was, forking my way carefully through a dark rich stew when I came across an intact jawbone. The row of tiny teeth gave it away. Perfect, they were very sharp and whiter than any in the dental ads.

I was in a bush restaurant of considerable repute in New Caledonia. Try the 'special' stew, the owner, a Frenchman born in the territory, had urged. It was a real treat. So I ordered it, and enjoyed it immensely. Made in the classic Gallic culinary tradition, it contained button mushrooms, bacon batons, small potatoes and lots of red wine. There was, though, a large number of very fine bones, and the amount of meat, though dark and very tasty, was small. And what was that faint aroma? The owner came to the table. Did I like it? Very much, I said, but why was it special? They didn't often get enough fruit bats to make it, he said.

Since then, I've eaten stewed bat one more time, in a resort restaurant in Honiara. Indeed, eating bats is quite common in the Pacific. They're rich in protein, and their small bones mostly disintegrate between the teeth—bonus calcium. And although I'd urge you to try stewed bat—I'm not sure that any of you would go for grilled or fried bat—I should warn you about their peculiar marinade. Bats hang upside-down most of the day and their toilet habits are, to say the least, lazy. I suppose it depends on the age of the bat, but, after a while, they inevitably begin to self-marinate. A light urinal whiff gets cooked into any stew made from them, matching, of course, the kind of delight Mr Leopold Bloom used to take in his breakfast kidney. (Joyce tells us in *Ulysses* that Mr Bloom loved 'stuffed roast heart' and 'fried hencod's roes'. But he especially delighted in his grilled breakfast kidneys of mutton, which gave to his palate, as Joyce put it, a 'fine tang of faintly scented urine'.)

In *Strange Foods*, Jerry Hopkins says that bats are popular in Asia as well as the Pacific islands. Their 'peculiarly pungent odour', as he puts it, can be alleviated by chillies, onions and garlic. But I would draw the line at the Saigon restaurant he once frequented that brought live bats to the table and slit their throats to produce a warm aperitif.

Steak tartare

Not all that unusual in 'safe' beef-producing countries such as Australia, steak tartare (raw beef with condiments) is highly dubious in much of the world. For health reasons, in fact, I'd be inclined not to order it in Europe, Africa or South America. Indeed, eat it once here and now in Australia and tick the box; as a food, it's becoming less safe by the year because of the possibility of a variation of mad cow disease that can infect humans.

Not so many years ago, raw beef could be trusted. I ate steak tartare for the first time at La Coupole, that quintessential Parisian bistro where timber chairs clattered on the tiled floor and the waiters had more attitude than a parliament of politicians. It was a house speciality there thirty years ago, and, as I recall, your large mound of finely ground fillet steak was topped with half an eggshell containing a yolk. Worcestershire sauce, mustard, ketchup, finely chopped shallots, chopped parsley, capers and one or two other supplements arrived in separate receptacles, and you composed the final flavour yourself. Some restaurants will do it for you under your direction, and you may taste it as you go.

Irrespective of its quality, raw beef has little flavour in itself; the condiments make it appetizing. Even when my mother threw me the odd cube of stewing steak as she hacked it to bits, I rolled it first in Cerebos. And ate it with raw onion arcs. I loved it that way, I have to admit, and in those days suffered no indigestion.

To die for

It might seem idiotic to get a restaurant to prepare for you a dish devoid of cooking, but it's mainly a question of safety; making customers ill is not good for business, and restaurants are bound to get it right. You *should* be able to trust a respectable restaurant's tartare. You'd have to know your butcher well before you'd make one at home.

An old French book I have lists four recipes for steak tartare, all used by reputable restaurants. After a preface recounting the tradition that 'Huns and Mongols', as it puts it, tenderized beef by putting it under their saddles, it says steak tartare is a winter dish, a tonic against the cold. It calls the humble hamburger a 'civilized' version of steak tartare. The four recipes work off the base given above. But an allegedly Greek derivative adds tomato paste, anchovy, garlic and cognac, and a 'Caucasian' version sees toast spread half-and-half with steak tartare and caviar (*see* 'Caviar'). I like the sound of it. And an Indian steak tartare contains curry, grated coconut and pine nuts.

Deep-fried mini-crabs

I've seen people leave a meal of crabs cut and bleeding. If the spikes don't get you the probes and pliers usually will. Without a doubt, crabs are the world's most frustrating food. Yet their sweet soft flesh is held in high repute. How do you get the taste and avoid the terror? Fly to Manila, where quite a while ago I ate the best crab platter I've consumed—before or since.

I was told, too, that it was more or less a renowned Filipino speciality, even if I suspect it might have been pretty hard on crab populations. (Unless, of course, there exists—possibly the case—a species of small crab ideal for this dish and their survival is under no threat.) And the dish? Nothing more nor less than what I'll have to call deep-fried mini-crabs. A plateful of whole cooked crabs arrived, tanned and crisp, on grey kitchen paper. The eating place in which

I tried this delight, by the way, was not a downmarket café in a far-flung village of a remote island. On the contrary, it was a very classy establishment in downtown Manila. Along one wall were stylish urns containing water with which you washed your hands after the crab dish.

It appeared as if the crabs, which were pretty flat and each only a small island in the palm of my hand, had been dusted in flour before frying. A source declared, in fact, that they are thrown live into a bag of flour, shaken—and possibly quite stirred—before the bag's contents are emptied into the boiling fat. I wasn't able to verify this explanation, but it's clear that some of the most appalling human behaviour produces some of humanity's most memorable eating. At any rate, you ate the lot; the claws and carapaces crunchy and fragile enough not to cause gum injuries. And they were amazingly sweet. As I recall now, not a single garnish of any sort accompanied them.

Some gourmets rave about our mud crabs, and, from my experience trapping them near Darwin, there appears to be absolutely no chance of their supply being exhausted. But I find them, as I do most crabs—particularly the ubiquitous blue swimmer and the giant from Bass Strait—fairly light in flavour and feeble in texture. And, according to some reliable sources, I understand muddies are chopped up alive for the pot in hundreds of restaurants Australia-wide every night.

I was a member of a small group of journalists who bought them cooked one day near Brisbane. We had worked hard on a colour supplement for more than a week and rewarded ourselves with a picnic on the beach—slab of beer, carton of muddies. The beer did what it usually does, and the crabs were only passable. As you do in such circumstances, we decided to alleviate the boredom by going for a bit of a paddle, even if it was a cool October day. One of our number, who has since gained a considerable journalistic reputation, categorically declined to join us in the surf. So we dragged him to the sand, ripped off his jeans, then his shoes and socks to reveal … bright pink toenails.

To die for

I think spanner crabs offer the best eating from the infraorder *Brachyura*. Partly it's because I'm just head over heels with their euphonious name (*Ranina ranina*), but mainly because their flesh is sweeter and more gelatinous than the others. Their huge domed shell also offers a surprising amount of meat, which is relatively easy to get at compared with the labour involved in ransacking their cousins. You will almost never be able to buy them anything other than freshly poached, but they're still good. Eat them with a proper mayonnaise or a herbed vinaigrette.

Andouillette at Chartier

I am frankly surprised at the soaring popularity of andouillette in French cafés. It seems to be threatening even the most popular Gallic *plats principaux*, such as steak and chips and veal blanquette. And I wonder why, because, despite their omnivorous reputation, some French still have qualms about andouillette.

It's the perfect dish to be squeamish about. An andouillette sausage is made from the bowels of pigs. When you split it open the most gorgeous smell of a blue-riband pigpen assaults your nostrils. As I wrote elsewhere once—it's my line so don't pinch it—the English name 'chitterlings' is a consonant off being appropriate.

And I'd urge you to eat your single andouillette in Chartier. (You will find andouillette throughout France, and you will rarely be served anything other than a good to excellent one.) I'm suggesting Chartier (7 rue du Faubourg-Montmartre) because I'm thinking of your pocket as well as the wonderful experience that eating in this place is. When I first lived in Paris, bistros like Chartier were not difficult to find. You've seen the scene in old Gallic movies— brass hat racks above French-polished alcoves, sometimes sawdust on the floor, decrepit black-and-white waiters in dark waistcoats and long white aprons, and isn't it cheap, cheap, cheap! Now there are few old-fashioned bistros, Chartier among the last. Yet in the 1890s it was one of a chain of similar bourgeois eating places. The cathedral-high ceiling is a skylight, and there are bevelled mirrors, polished stone wainscoting, wood panels and a lovely rural mural. Parisians and tourists pour daily through Chartier by the hundreds, getting more than their money's worth from a long list of standard bistro fare.

Chartier's andouillette is a very plump sausage, pale fawn in colour. When you run a knife along it, curls of guts tumble out. The accompaniment is chips and dijon mustard. Some of us—I was one—fell in love early with the whiff of urine in food. Perhaps we were bed-wetters. ('There's nothing wrong with a boy who wets his bed,' old Dr Galbraith said sagely. 'But not from the top of his wardrobe!' said my mother ... Only joking.) I loved kidneys, for instance.

No matter how scrupulously you clean offal involved in the endgame of digestion, animal wastes continue to play a part in what is produced from them. On this very point I sought expert opinion from my brother-in-law the millionaire French butcher. The entrails of pigs, he assured me, were scrupulously and meticulously scrubbed under fresh cold running water to make andouillette. Washed to within a millimetre of their lives, he might have added.

Cassoulet from Castelnaudary

If we're going to be tawdry, try a cassoulet from Castelnaudary. It's basically pork and beans, but it's also France's heartiest main course. Remember the westerns? Unshaven and filthy, Humphrey Bogart and his band of dreamers sit around their campfire in some godforsaken crevice in the Sierra Madre. They're eating with their mouths open and talking gold at the same time. Their forks tattoo tinnily on the plates. 'We'll find it!' spits Humph. 'There's gold out there, I tell you!' further expectorating, and jumping to his feet. He waves his arms.

'Everywhere!' He sits down, drawing close to the fire. Lowering his voice to a grumble, he looks disdainfully at his plate. 'There'll be no more of this ...'—hurling the plate into the sagebrush—'goddamned pork and beans!'

Of course, I doubt if Hollywood's caterers ever produced really great pork and beans. And that's all cassoulet is. *Great* pork and beans. To do it properly takes time and effort. No special cooking skills are needed. I've done it a handful of times and weep in pleasure at the results. After eating it, I often wish I'd been there with Humph and the boys, the skinny kid by the rock in the left of frame. And I'd swallow nervously and drag a canister from my saddle bag and say something like, 'Excuse me, boss, but me mamma packed me a *fancy* pork and beans. It's called cassoulet, boss, and it sure tastes swell.' (I suppose I'd then need to take cover.)

Said to be the home of cassoulet, Castelnaudary is a town in the southern Languedoc region of France near Spain. *Larousse Gastronomique* has almost three columns of small type on the dish. And there are, of course, many versions of it. So go to Castelnaudary, scout about, and determine the best cassoulet restaurants. (I don't have a particular recommendation, having passed through the town only once long ago. We stumbled by luck on a very good cassoulet outlet.)

Cassoulet used to be cooked in an earthenware pot, reports *Larousse*, called a *cassole d'Issel*, from whence cometh its name. And serious food writers—as opposed to frivolous ones, presumably—recognize that there are actually three separate versions of cassoulet originating in Castelnaudary, Toulouse and Carcassonne, which are all close. The Castelnaudary version has fresh pork, ham, knuckle of pork and bacon rind and is always mentioned first. That of Carcassonne adds mutton and partridges to the above, and the Toulouse spin adds breast of pork as well as sausage, mutton and confit-style preserved goose or duck legs. Overkill, if you like.

The traditional recipes require you to follow a very lengthy procedure involving simmering haricot beans with aromatic vegetables, garlic, tomato purée, seasoning and the meats. I'm shortening the procedure, but when it's almost cooked you cover the surface of your cassoulet—which should be cooked in a clay pot—with breadcrumbs and goose fat and put it in a baker's oven 'heated with mountain furze'. (I can see Humph grinning with delight. 'You're right, son! That mountain furze makes all the difference!'). It must be baked gently for several hours. The crust that forms on top should be stirred back into the cassoulet two or three times and the dish should be served from the pot in which it is cooked.

If I remember rightly, Humph and the boys never found gold. Now if their pork and beans had been cassoulet ...

Herrings in oil at the Grand Colbert

Even in France they're called simply 'herrings in oil', yet this classic dish is one of my favourite starters. Provided we could lay our hands on the finest smoked herring fillets, we could easily try it at home. But I suspect that not even the Parisian restaurant at which I'm going to suggest you taste them, Grand Colbert (2 rue Vivienne), would smoke its own fish. Food is all about beginning with the best produce, and if someone else specializes in producing sublime makings then why not let them.

Herrings undoubtedly remain prodigious in number, judging by the ubiquitousness of kippers and other concoctions that use them. They congregate from spring to autumn in enormous shoals in French Atlantic coastal waters. Catching them in quantity over a couple of months at the end of the northern autumn has had to mean, of course, salting and smoking them. After they're salted, herrings are usually cold-smoked—hung some distance from the fire to incorporate the odour and flavour of the smoke at fairly low temperatures. Beech wood is preferred.

Once you've procured your smoked herring fillets, turning them into 'harengs à l'huile' shouldn't cause you too much grief. You soak them in milk or a mixture of milk and water for at least an hour and sometimes even longer to remove most of the salt. Then you dry them and pack them into a terrine, alternating the fillets with layers of onion arcs, carrot discs, broken-up bay leaves and generous sprigs of thyme. (No salt, of course, but I can't see why you couldn't add peppercorns.) Pour fine olive oil on top and leave the fish to marinate for at least twenty-four hours in a cool place (but not the refrigerator). Indeed, herring fillets can marinate for several days, the use-by date arriving after about a week.

And I'm suggesting that you let the Grand Colbert do it for you because they've made the dish something of a spectacular. The fillets arrive in an earthenware terrine big enough to serve a good Catholic family and all its extensions. The oil is clear, the carrot discs, onion arcs and sprigs of thyme generous. And you just help yourself. Hop in. Gorge, if you like, while you take in the Colbert's wonderful nineteenth-century style—the mosaic floor, orb lights, stained glass, mirrors, and show posters. You'll feel that what you're doing is special. And it is.

Foie gras in Bordeaux

Fascinated by memories, I am sure that some of our best simply lose their correct places in the files of our minds. They become so precious to us that they take on a ubiquitous universality or get lost in a special covert. Exactly when they occurred is the least remembered thing about them. Such a phenomenon has clouded my recollecting exactly the date—or even the season or the year—of my most treasured foie gras eat. But this is not a philosophy text, and having cleared my throat, let me say a few more pertinent words about this greatest of foods.

It would be the first course on my last menu. And, here again, life is complicated, because it's produced from the private agony of animals. Ducks and geese are shut up in the dark and force-fed grain for the last weeks of their lives. Their diseased livers—swollen to up to ten times' normal size—are foie gras. Now, I am one hundred per cent behind you if you decline ever to touch the stuff. Perhaps I should decline, too. It's a question that crosses my mind every time I eat it. But I eat it, and perhaps I should be only ashamed, not delighted. There are no excuses, and my only explanation for my consumption of foie gras is that it is sublime and life is short. Moreover, there is accounting for nothing once we are dead.

In September 2004, the French agriculture ministry defied its partners in a united Europe by giving the 6000 producers of foie gras an extra five years—until 2010—to do without the cramped cages in which geese and ducks are confined towards the end of their fattening. I am indebted to a London *Guardian* report for what follows. The ministry argued that the European Union could recommend but not prescribe. Under pressure from more ethically gastronomic countries than France, many European organizations have in recent years attempted to end the production of foie gras. But France produces some seventy per cent of the 20 000 tonnes of it made annually worldwide. It is also responsible for about eighty-five per cent of global consumption. To fatten the birds, corn is forced through a tube down their throat three times a day for the last month of the birds' lives. At slaughter, these animals have—as well as acute liver disease—diarrhoea, waddling problems, lesions, inflammations and panting.

At a time in the distant past I can't now actually specify, my wife and I and one of our sons, who was a baby at the time, stayed overnight at Magescq, a small town south of Bordeaux on the road to Spain. It's foie gras country around here, and the delightful hotel in which we put up was already known for its simple fine cooking. Indeed, I think the Relais de la Poste had by then already won a Michelin star. (By 2000 it had two.) For a very reasonable price we were shown to a huge upstairs bedroom in a modern chalet-like building in the middle of lawns and large pines. It was furnished sun-king style, the chairs, bed and writing table all in centuries-old carved fruitwoods. The management provided a cot for the kid, and also an electronic device that would broadcast his crying at our dinner table if he woke up. (It can't have been so long ago.) And we went down to dinner.

And I had duck foie gras, the Relais's speciality. If you look at recent Michelin guides, you will notice that the Relais lists it as an offering that is garnished with *girolles*, a wonderful small wild mushroom. As I recall, on this night three or four huge slices of liver—a ploughman's serving, or, in Bordeaux, perhaps that should be a pruner's serving—arrived on a simple salad of frizzy lettuce. They sat in a slick of cooking juices deglazed with red wine vinegar. And I ate heaven. Lightly rubbery on the outside, foie gras has an inner texture somewhere between the barest gelatinousness and curdled cream. It is rich beyond belief. Taste? You'll have to eat some.

Many years later, the night after we had Pierre-Yves's brochettes of blackbirds and thrushes (*see* 'Pierre-Yves' brochettes ...'), we ate foie gras. That afternoon, we had driven for an hour to a wholesaler Collette habitually bought from and trusted. And we had come home with really too much foie gras for four. But we cooked it nonetheless. Or, rather, I was asked to cook it. The other three daringly avowed that they would not trust themselves with it.

Mainly pale fawn but with the slightest tinge of pink, foie gras lobes are about the size of a toddler's mini-Aussie Rules football. Uncooked, the liver has a texture somewhere between soft wax and playdough. And I cut several large slices and tried to reproduce what I had eaten at the Relais (and seen done once or twice before in restaurant kitchens, I should add). I fried the slices very quickly, beginning with a little butter in the pan. A minute or three on the first side, half that time on the second. Foie gras throws so much fat that after frying half-a-dozen slices of it clear liquid grease was just about overflowing the pan. Collette kept it, of course, for other cooking, and I made a sauce out of perhaps half a cup of it and vinegar.

Closer to home is a foie gras dish the equal of any I have tried. It's at Gaddi's, Hong Kong's top restaurant by a fair margin. Philip Sedgwick, its British chef in 2004, has created something of timeless gastronomic value. A thick puck of cold tight goose-liver terrine wears a cloak of transparent sweet–sour wine jelly the colour of a shallow sea on a sunny morning. Halves of pipped and peeled green grapes are set in the jelly. The degrees of gelatinousness are brilliant. The liver itself adds amazing butteriness, but also contributes a balancing light bitterness. Accompanying is a copse of superlative tiny greens, a blob of dense old balsamic vinegar and a slice of brioche toast.

You'll notice that Philip's creation uses cold foie gras, which is the way most people eat it in restaurants. The lobes are packed tightly into a terrine and baked in a bain-marie. After cooling, it's refrigerated and served in slices. Don't be tempted by 'foie gras' products in cans. Most of them actually contain very little fattened liver. Read the labels very carefully for their contents if you really feel you have to buy these corruptions. We can't get fresh foie gras in Australia, so you must eat it on your next European adventure. But I'll respect you in the morning if you don't. Significantly!

Cod at Casa Labra

I grew up hating New Zealand and all who populated her. It was the cod that did it, you understand, those despicable orange-coloured flanks of fish that crossed the Tasman in shallow paling boxes. It was the only fish we ever saw at my house. The only fish my mother cooked. Mind you, we had it only once a year. Not only was Good Friday imbued with mournful spiritualism for Methodists, but we had to eat cod as well. It was the only Friday of the year many good Proddies went Catholic and declined red meat. So my mother would go out and buy it, poaching it for dinner. And it was *so* salty and *so* flavourless. And the way the flesh flaked away in bits from the absolutely repellent skin, which in itself made me gag, just added to the awful chore of having to eat it. (Although chipping away the flakes was fun in a gastro-technical way.)

Many years later I learned that on Good Fridays I'd been eating an approximation of the great Mediterranean delicacy 'bacalao', as they call it in Spain, or 'baccala', as it's known in Italy. I say an approximation, because Kiwi cod was never dried as this species—or something like it—is in the Mediterranean. And possibly because it wasn't dried and crusted with salt, no-one in Australian households thought to soak the salt out of it before cooking. Bacalao is soaked in water to remove excess salt. Indeed, an Italian reference I've consulted says dried cod should be soaked for twenty-four hours, the water changed three or four times.

In Madrid, Casa Labra, a restaurant almost a century-and-a-half old, specializes in dried salted cod, at any rate, serving half-a-dozen bacalao dishes at any given moment. (Hundreds of recipes exist.) And I suggest that you get there and try a great delicacy. Mind you, this tiny place of frosted glass, huge saffron napkins and fine blonde joinery is better known for its adjoining tapas bar. A world away, it's a noisy walk-up joint where you have to battle through three-deep locals to order a sherry. (It's here, by the way, that Pablo Iglesias founded the Spanish socialist party more than a century ago.)

I tried bacalao two ways. (You'll notice immediately when *you* do that there will be an almost total lack of saltiness.) Apart from a saline mouthful or two at the thick end of one fillet, the fish itself had fine subtle flavour and a kind of light plasticity. Its neutrality, of course, was a blank gastro-canvas on which to paint other flavour-colours. One fillet, for instance, was topped with tanned fried shavings of garlic, more deeply tanned rings of fried red chilli, chopped parsley and a slick of olive oil. The other arrived under a sauce of medium starchiness that had a firm tomato base and was studded with capers and lots of oyster mushrooms. Both were very good.

I came away inspired, determined to give New Zealand cod another go. I'm thinking of trying pepper cod flamed in cognac, cod with a vinaigrette or beurre blanc—even cod with a classic brown sauce or under a warm gazpacho. Who knows? They might work.

Joel Robuchon's mashed potato

Joel Robuchon was France's star chef of the 1980s. At his restaurant Jamin, in Paris, he created simple but stratospherically refined dishes that shook the world. He claimed that all one needed to do in a kitchen was to make a carrot taste like a carrot. Of course, there was more to it than that. Robuchon's famous creamy cauliflower soup, for instance, had a precise ring of caviar eggs around its rim, and a rich dark caviar jelly in a separate layer beneath it. (And it was fabulous.) His crème brûlée was riddled with the 'dust'—actually they're seeds—from vanilla pods. (And it was magnificent.) But of all his creations, his potato purée was talked about most. It was snowy white, had the consistency of finishing plaster yet an unbelievable richness. And those of us who mashed potatoes regularly in home kitchens wondered how he did it. We weren't to find out easily. One cataclysmic day in 1995, Robuchon retired early, just like that, a rich man. He wrote a newspaper column and consulted, but he wasn't going back to the burners.

But I got the secret to the Robuchon mash quite by accident in Sydney, oddly enough. Before I let you in on it, though, I had better explain that when a French chef reaches superstar status he no longer actually cooks. I interviewed Robuchon after lunch service and his tunic and long white apron were impeccable—not a single spatter or spill sullied them. His navy trousers were beautifully cut from rich cloth, creases impeccable, and his expensive black slip-ons were highly buffed. A chef at this level oversees and shouts at underlings, you understand ... doesn't get his hands actually dirty.

One of his most talented cooks—a bloke who *did* the work in the Jamin kitchen—was for several years executive chef of a Sydney five-star hotel. (He then went on to work in Tokyo.) And I asked him one day for the secret to Robuchon's mash. He laughed heartily and said, '*Beaucoup de beurre!*' It was just lots and lots of butter that made it famous, he confided.

But being a Robuchon concoction, the potatoes would have been of a special sort possessing magnificent flavour, and the butter, equally, would have been the best that the great man's money could buy. The former Jamin cook also explained that the potatoes were first baked in their skins, not boiled. With a bit of care, however, I believe you could make an approximation to the Robuchon mash at home.

Either that or taste the real thing, because Robuchon has made a comeback. Not only has he fairly recently opened a classy restaurant in Macau, but he has set up L'Atelier de Joel Robuchon (roughly translatable as 'Joel's workshop') in Paris and Tokyo. And web references suggest strongly that the Robuchon mash is a must. I couldn't imagine it wouldn't be. Eat it, and be astonished that boring mashed spud can be smoother and richer than a Hollywood cosmetic surgeon.

Pettavel pigeon

Pigeon has come a long way from the days when Ernest Hemingway—of great and ponderous literary cast—used to say he pounced on them in the middle of Paris. You can't trust fiction writers to tell the truth, of course, and shadows of doubt fall over his assertion. (I think he even threw a few of those shadows himself.) But, if his claim is true, I don't think the town-hall variety of the genus *Columba* would be especially tasty, given the ends of dead sandwiches they consume.

On the other hand, I've eaten sublime pigeon in restaurants. Indeed, it's my favourite bird. And the best I've tasted—one you *must* try before you die— is served at Pettavel Winery and Restaurant west of Geelong. It's partly the bird and partly the wonderful cooking that this place consistently turns out. The poultry itself is said to be a 'boned wild Barossa pigeon'. But it comes from a highly reputable South Australian supplier, so I presumed when I ate it first in mid-2002 that it had been fed and fattened. Even so, a whole quartered pigeon arrived on a super-pungent, fungal glaze condensed from porcini mushrooms. And its flesh was left underdone, succulent but chewy near the bone, tender in the big muscles, sweet, liverish and bright pink. It was fabulous, transcendental, promoting a magical blend of mineral, animal and vegetable flavours. Fried slippery jack mushrooms and a tower of creamy gratin-dauphinois-style potato accompanied.

I'm told that the chefs at Pettavel plate their pigeon in several different ways, and I can't promise you that you can order it as I ate it. But order it anyway. You won't be disappointed.

Pigeon dishes seem to stamp themselves in my memory. At the wonderful Claude's in Sydney, former chef-owner Tim Pak Poy once presented me and a small group of visiting Japanese journalists with what he called 'woods' pigeon, which was also from South Australia. As I recall, the claws and head were retained, and the birds were pretty much as good as Pettavel's, perhaps a little firmer in texture. I tied Tim to a chair and applied cruel and unusual punishment, but he revealed nothing about how he got them, where they were from, if they'd been fed. Chefs are sometimes like that with great produce. He said only that they had been caught in forests—netted?

Most pigeon for the plate is squab. By definition, these birds are from twenty-eight to thirty-two days old. They have never left the nest and are fed secret blends of pellets and grains. I toured a pigeon-grower's coops in the Yarra Valley once, not too far from Melbourne. I saw fluffy bundles of listless pale-grey joy about the size of a good melon just sitting around in their nests, which were on shelves in dim slab huts. They got fed, and cooed only occasionally. A light agricultural smell pervaded all. Pigeons might be filthy—at Trafalgar Square these days you're warned against skidding—but their gastronomic value is amazing. What surprises me most about them is how such sedentary poultry can have such dark and delicious flesh. It must be in the breeding. Usually, dark-fleshed birds tell of action—high metabolic rates and complex networks of blood distribution. Unlike smaller or larger poultry, pigeons are able to marry their sweetness to an intense cooked bloodiness. For poultry their size, too, they retain an excellent gelatinous texture.

If you want to roast them at home, go for a simple stuffing of milk-soaked bread with finely chopped smoked bacon, an egg and fresh herbs. (Things like smashed garlic and other aromatics are optional, of course.) You'll get a better result if you tie the legs and wings tightly to the body. Roast them with a lot of butter, putting them in a very hot oven to start. Baste them often. No more than half an hour does it. Roasted squab goes with most vegetables.

Tim's snow eggs

Speaking of Tim Pak Poy, his take on snow eggs is arguably the most important recent contribution to Australian cooking. I think it's crucial in a world sense. It's a huge culinary leap forward in an intellectual way, the model for what I've called—in an earlier book—'narrative cooking'. Tim's approach is revolutionary; don't be fooled that what chefs are doing overseas is more important or avant-garde. It isn't. If you want to say you've done the gastronomic equivalent of smashing the atom or understanding Stephen W. Hawking's physical union of time and space then eat Tim's snow eggs. They are vital to the development of cuisine.

Traditional snow eggs are whipped whites of egg set quickly in sugared milk. The milk is the base for a crème anglaise (a liquid sugared cream) in which the eggs float. Tim uses the idea for the eggs in what is a savoury dish, not a dessert.

First, he folds mud-crab flesh through the egg whites, a brilliant idea. The whites are turned into 'set' protein clouds by poaching in what he calls 'crab milk', an infusion of crustacean into milk that has also been flavoured with truffles. A single snow egg sits on a salad of crabmeat and shreds of truffle and its dressing. And if all that sounds fairly orthodox if somewhat extravagant, what comes next is the surprise. The other elements of the dish include what he calls a 'crispbread-like' filigree made principally from high-quality, very bitter chocolate. But there is also bitter melon done two ways—salted and fried, and simply blanched. Most of the dish's action occurs between the chocolate and the snow eggs, which are widely separated on the sweet–bitter axis. And, as Tim put it to me one day, when you begin to eat the dish sweetness is evident in the crab, and bitterness in the melon. But this is the key point: the filigree melts and runs through the dish and into the sauce in the bottom of the bowl, which itself becomes richer and more bitter. And, in Tim's words, 'you wonder what's going on'.

There is genius in this offering, because for the first time (that I'm aware of), a temporal element has been built into a kitchen creation. In short, the flavours the dish delivers change over time. That's why I've aligned the dish with storytelling, and I hope Tim pushes the idea as far as it can go in the years ahead. Until the middle of 2004 Tim might have cooked you snow eggs at Claude's. But after ten years as owner and sixteen overall in the restaurant, he has sold out.

To die for

Zuni chicken

On the cusp of the 1990s, I decided to see what the Californian fuss was all about. Californian 'cuisine' was being talked up everywhere. So I spent two weeks in Los Angeles and San Francisco, trying the most esteemed restaurants on the West Coast. I'll admit I went with some prejudice—as legal eagles never want to admit they have by heading their letters 'without prejudice'. I knew just how good the quickly developing Australian cooking was, and believed only American cultural clout and high marketing skills made Californian cuisine known worldwide. I'll admit, too, that I was a little indignant: nothing could be as good as what we were doing in Australia, I thought. I was able to say precisely what Australian cooking was, but wondered if a definition existed for Californian cuisine.

I left the West Coast disappointed. Not only could no-one tell me what characterized the so-called Californian cooking, but most of the alleged top places I ate at were pretty ordinary, in my view. Their food failed to dance. One restaurant—one dish—stood out. It was the signature wood-roasted chicken of Zuni Café in Market Street, San Francisco, where Judy Rodgers was mining her kitchen experience at Troisgros in Roanne (*see* 'Salmon with sorrel') and with Alice Waters in San Francisco itself. The Zuni chook was wonderful. I liked it so much I went back the following night, only to have an expensive leather jacket stolen from the front seat of a friend's car. (Young men carrying baseball bats could be seen patrolling the streets that night and the passenger window had received a mighty whack. I hope someone is wearing my jacket still. It is by the famed French maker McDouglas so will last you a lifetime. Make sure you look after it!)

The secret was salt, Judy told me. A day before, if I remember rightly, her chickens were salted, especially inside the carcasses. Using salt to draw out water and thereby concentrate flavour is a grand culinary principle (*see* 'Fried eggplant'). Then chopped fresh herbs in olive oil were inserted under the skin. The chickens are roasted to order—you wait for something like forty-five minutes—in a wood-fired oven that dominates the restaurant's ground floor, and your finished bird is strewn in pieces on a Tuscan bread salad. Judy said her influences were mainly Mediterranean, and I see from Internet entries that the salad includes radicchio these days. (I had a feeling the ones I ate were pretty much green.)

Despite having eaten Zuni chicken twice, I can't recall in great detail what the salad included, so gastronomically domineering was the poultry. But I remember cubes of garlic-rubbed toast, or perhaps fried bread, pine nuts and dried vine fruit, perhaps sultanas or muscatels.

I prepare the dish from memory fairly often at home, even if I am without a wood-fired oven. I soak the vine fruit in port or another spirituous wine from northern Victoria (tokay is terrific), and add the juice to olive oil and lemon juice to make a dressing for the salad. I try to base the salad on as many sorts of leaves and fresh herbs from the garden as possible. The herbs mirror those that I've slid under the skin of the chicken. The result is always sublime, and I thank Judy for the salting tip.

Vincisgrassi—a simple lasagne

I'm not about to apologize for the offal dishes in this book. You will have noticed them from time to time. This one is absolutely sublime, but it has a single very important advantage over the others; you don't know you're eating the brains and glands of animals. But you'll be wondering, all the same, just why Valerio Nucci's vincisgrassi is so rich and creamy, so smooth and comforting, so delectable in the seductiveness of its unction. It's because of the offal.

To die for

Prince Windischgratz, I am told, was an Austrian general at a time when Austrian generals were aristocrats, rode around on horses and wore funny hats with lots of feathers. They probably fought Italians and liked the local food. This dish, from central Italy, was named after him. Just why is lost in history. But in Melbourne it has been transformed by Valerio into a sublime concoction that you can catch, as they say in theatrical circles, most lately at The Grand Hotel in Burnley Street, Richmond. (There are so many Grand hotels, most of them insignificant.)

Valerio and his sous chef, Leonardo Gelsomino, the man who does the work, first make fresh pasta with an added nip of dry fortified wine. Then they fry the usual aromatic suspects—carrots, onions and celery—in butter and olive oil. They wait for all this virtually to caramelize before chucking in good chuck steak, which is the foundation protein of the sauce. They seal and brown the surfaces of the meat before adding white wine, bay leaves, cloves, mild streaky bacon that adds a lot of pork fat, and dried ham. This might braise away quite happily for ninety minutes or more, until, at any rate, it breaks down and the meat is soft and crumbling. They chop the contents of the pan very finely and stew it again, this time with a house-made tomato sauce.

Meanwhile, they work on brains and sweetbreads, cleaning them, removing filaments and soaking in water and vinegar to whiten them and remove any traces of blood. The offal is diced and put into the sauce. The Latin gentlemen then compose their béchamel, the culinary cement that glues lasagne together (among its many purposes), flavouring the basic ingredients of butter, flour and milk with bay leaves and cloves.

And when all that is done, the lasagne is assembled. There are four layers of pasta, lots of sauce and béchamel in between them, knobs of butter, which gives the concoction succulence, and grated parmesan on top. It's baked for around thirty-five minutes in a moderate oven, and is exquisite. In a single paragraph the first time I reviewed it I hailed its 'melting creamy cheesiness [and] wonderful sweetness'. It became an ensemble that was 'unctuously sublime'. Words only—and someone ought to lock me away occasionally from computers—but I meant every syllable of it. You'll believe me when you eat it.

Poached egg and truffled polenta

You cook the ingredients you've got. Paul Wilson, a significant chef, one day had a surfeit of truffled polenta. And from the oversupply he created only a few years ago one of Australia's best restaurant dishes.

Briton Paul came to Melbourne in the 1990s to run a snazzy new brasserie in the freshly renovated department store Georges. A retail icon where the nicest people shopped, Georges also stocked luxury foods. But one day someone over-ordered an Italian brand of polenta (cornmeal) containing dried truffles. It was what Paul Wilson calls a 'gimmicky product', but it had a good nose, as the wine guys say. (The floral fungi infused the polenta.) It simply wasn't marching out the door; that was the problem. Especially at Georges' prices.

It was a pity not to use the stuff, and Paul had an obvious outlet in the brasserie. In London restaurants, he had been taught to use truffles simply—slice them over pasta or free-range eggs. And he came up with a terrifically simple way of using the excess polenta. Why not just put a poached egg on top, add some truffle slices and a wafer of parmesan cheese? Paul says it came up well first time.

When Georges failed, Paul took the dish to radii, a restaurant in the Hyatt hotel chain. Mostly because of the dish and the attention it drew to Paul's immaculate cooking, radii quickly became Melbourne's top brasserie. Twice a year the restaurant received fresh truffles from Europe and they were stored in the freezer in polenta, which was used in the signature dish. And by 2004, Paul had moved to the Botanical Hotel in South Yarra, where the truffled polenta and poached egg remains an obligatory inclusion on the food list.

These days the perfumed polenta is cooked with parmesan, garlic and cream. A warm poached egg is placed on top, and freshly shaved truffles nestle on the egg. Balancing on the lot is a very thin slice of parmesan—so thin, in fact, that it appears to be a sheet of pasta. Then over the lot goes a truffle-infused classic beurre blanc (*see* 'A proper beurre blanc').

It's super-rich, this dish, but oh so creamy and smooth in the mouth. You'd be mad not to squeeze it into your life's menu at least once.

Philippe Mouchel's chicken-liver gateau

Philippe Mouchel made his name in Australia as the chef who made the great Paul Bocuse's name in Australia. Complicated? Not really, once you realize that Philippe was the man who did the cooking at Bocuse's French headquarters near Lyons before repeating the dose in Melbourne. For six years from 1991 Bocuse in Melbourne produced the best classic Gallic cooking Victoria had seen. It was perfect, exemplified by such things as slices of beef fillet sandwiching an equal-sized puck of braised beef cheek in a sticky, deeply flavoured sauce. A lightly salted disc of bone marrow topped the lot.

After Bocuse closed, Philippe moved on to lesser ventures in Melbourne and Sydney before returning to Japan, where he had worked as an executive chef before. But now he and his Japanese wife and children are back in Melbourne. I hope they stay.

And he'd be the first to tell you that the sublime chicken-liver 'gateau' served at his eponymous brasserie on the banks of the Yarra is not his creation. In fact, he informs me, it was almost certainly one of the early nouvelle cuisine dishes. (*See* 'Salmon with sorrel' for another.) Philippe thinks that the late, great Alain Chapel probably originated it some time in the 1960s at his restaurant at Mionnay, where I once ate his celebrated mushroom cappuccino and followed it up with roasted guinea fowl speckled with lead shot. (You could either spit out the shot or add it to your fillings.)

Like many great works of culinary art, the gateau is extremely simple. It was the thinking up of it in the first place that was difficult. I have no doubt that if Chapel was around he would tell us so. (A dogmatic man, he didn't much like journalists. He once upbraided me for quizzing him on the effects of journalism on cooking. There was only one true cooking, he thundered. It was '*bonne*', and it was served at a table around which *convives* sat on comfortable chairs, shared the food and talked.) By the time Philippe became acquainted with it, Bocuse and several other leading chefs in the Lyons area were cooking the dish. Among them would have been Georges Blanc, who has an official role in certificating the famous yellow Bresse chickens.

Bresse chickens, paradoxically, produce an almost white liver, which was used by French chefs for the gateau. And the gateau itself is basically just a cooked mousse. Philippe marinates the livers in milk overnight to whiten them and remove the last traces of blood. Then they're blended with whole eggs, bone marrow and milk infused with garlic, the result pressed through a very fine sieve into moulds. The moulds are poached in a bain-marie for about thirty minutes in a cool oven. The result is transcendentally fine, a tawny turret with the faintest of pink interiors. Let me quote from my observations in a recent review: 'To take your spoon and slice through its fawn duco to reveal the palest and smoothest of interior pinks is one of Melbourne's great eating experiences.' Once it's in your mouth, you'll taste a 'wonderfully intense but softened liverishness and a uniformly sleek gentle-jelly texture'.

In Melbourne, Philippe garnishes the gateau with lentil purée studded with carrot dice and strips of crisp bacon. It's to keep costs down. In central France it's usually served with a creamy yabby bisque.

To die for

Open lasagne of artichoke and gorgonzola

People think I'm full up to pussy's bow—as the saying used to go—with great food. They think that, because I'm a restaurant reviewer, I must eat brilliantly all the time. I do, in fact, eat a lot of great tucker. But I also eat a lot that is well below par.

But I reckon restaurant dishes should be magical. All the time. Chefs have access to the best produce and the best equipment. And they're also supposed to have all the culinary techniques that allow them to cook something that well and truly transcends what can be turned out of a domestic kitchen. Yet only very occasionally do I find myself eating something that represents consummate culinary conjuring.

Such a dish was Rick Mikus's open lasagne of artichoke and gorgonzola. It was sublime, stunning, and Rick is no longer chef at Sud in Melbourne where I ate it. (Since then, too, Sud has had two changes of ownership.) He is still around town, though, and we shall just have to find him and inveigle him into doing it all over again.

His lasagne was beguilingly simple, but the ingredients were great and the dish's conception approached artistic perfection. Essentially, three large sheets of fresh house-made pasta were folded to handkerchief size and piled in a bowl with cross-sections of small artichoke. Left loose, Rick felt that they constituted an 'open' pasta instead of the tightly structured conventional favourite. A few sweated rocket leaves were strewn on top, and the lot bathed in clear but richly flavoured cooking juices haunted by gorgonzola.

In the early days of Sud, which produced some of Melbourne's best Latin food, the menus changed almost daily. Rick and his sous chef were forced to wrack their brains to come up with new culinary creations. It is under such pressure that greatness flourishes.

Rick's fresh pasta was produced from semolina, olive oil, eggs and flour. He can't remember exactly when, why, or how he conceived the inspired artichoke–gorgonzola partnership, but it came. He regularly had small globe artichokes, which he stripped back so that no woodiness remained, retaining a length of stalk. Habitually, he blanched them and preserved them in brine.

The open lasagne was made to order. He pan-fried a little garlic and chilli in olive oil then brought his preserved artichokes up to temperature in the pan. Once hot, the pan and its contents were deglazed with a glug or three of South Australian riesling. The trick—as with all vinous additions—was not to add too much. (Many chefs fail to understand this.)

Three imperfectly square pasta sheets that had already been partly cooked went in next, then just the right amount of gorgonzola. He had to work fast so that the cheese would melt but not react to its treatment by turning bitter, its blue arteries hardening to unappetizing squiggles. A handful of parsley went last.

To assemble the dish, Rick took a sheet from the pan, added some sauce, laid down a second sheet, more sauce, and finally the third and the remains of the sauce. Rocket garnished. Now, where is that man?

Fricassee of the pig

Gary Jones loves his culinary heritage so much that his email address is 'blackpudding'. He comes from the grey grimy north of England, and his father was 'down pit'. But he didn't become a scientist, a football player or a miner—he could have, because he was good at study and sport and his father was already in the local business. For no apparent reason, Gary became a chef. It wasn't something Yorkshire lads did, but Gary liked cooking and thought he'd try his luck at catering college. After graduating and working at Claridge's in London and several fine French kitchens, he became a very good chef. Soon, he was one of Britain's finest, making London's Groucho Club famous for its food in the early 1980s. Then he came to Australia and did it all over again here.

He worked in or owned several top restaurants in Melbourne and Perth, including Western Australia's best, San Lorenzo. (These days he is an executive chef in Queensland.) But in most restaurants he has had, he listed a dish of great wonderment: his fricassee of the pig.

Very rarely does a culinary creation tell you much about the person who conceived it. But Gary Jones's fricassee—in a similar way to Cheong Liew's four dances (see 'Four dances of the sea')—is a kind of culinary autobiography.

Chefs often talk passionately about how they invented a dish, the circumstances of its coming to them. Almost never do they write their thoughts down in any other way than a dreary catalogue of ingredients and an even more turgid procedure. (God, cookbooks are tedious!) When I asked Gary to write down the how-to of the fricassee for me I wasn't sure what to expect. I knew it would be different, but I thought there was a good chance it would need a little 'sexing up', as they say about most formal British reports. Reading what he wrote brought tears to my eyes. Let me quote it almost verbatim. A warning: you'll need tissues. Behold peptic poetry.

Before the dish there were the memories—my grandmother's cooking on an open coal-fired stove. Pigs' trotters were frequently cooked, boiled with fresh vegetables on the open fire then into a side-oven to cook slowly for hours, the pig's head broken and cooked the same way. The choice bits were the succulent cheeks and tongue, the ears stripped of their flesh eaten with mustard. The memory also of the pig's blood mixed with lots of onion and apple cooked in an old cake tin in the coal-fired oven when the embers were at their lowest. This was real food for real working men. It wasn't the cholesterol or heart disease that killed them but the dust from forty-five years working at the coalface, and, yes, there was plenty of animal fat. The bubble 'n' squeak had to be cooked in the dripping from the roast.

Never once did I see all these things on the one plate, but years later the memories became an idea. A few changes and a dish was born to make New Labour proud. The pigs' trotters became stuffed ... The black pudding nothing changed, except that the cake tin was replaced by a Le Creuset terrine. The pigs' ears were crumbed and fried after long slow cooking for texture, and the pigs' cheeks were slightly fried. The bubble 'n' squeak was refined—potatoes baked and buttered with diced bacon. This was not a dish to seduce but a dish to arouse the passions. It was and always will be a dish for fond memories of a bygone age.

Dear, oh dear, doesn't that make most of the efforts of our star literary chefs and food writers seem feeble? Just before I hand over to Gary to write the rest of the book, let me say that the elements of the fricassee—a large counter of black pudding, plinth of cheek, cylinders of trotter and perfect spoonful of bubble 'n' squeak—were positioned in an absolutely limpid lake of sticky, golden veal reduction. It was a dish to die for. Quite simply to die for! Book Gary to cook it on your way out.

Fish sandwich from a pitching Bosphorus fishing boat

In some ways, Istanbul is a world gastronomic centre. It's not that Turkish cuisine has any more or fewer merits than others from the Levant—or elsewhere, for that matter. It's simply that Istanbul is at a cultural crossroads, and that means trade of all kinds passes through it, and always has. Especially trade in commodities.

So you may see in its spice market a blinding variety of condiments with which to flavour food. Displayed in all manner of containers, their colours alone would drive a painter insane with envy. And you will also see caviar at some of the world's best prices. (At least when compared with their Australian and European counterparts.)

But I would insist that you visit Istanbul at least once before you die, not just for its spice market or, indeed, its sublime architectural monuments and history. (You can feel, for instance, the mysterious troubled crest formed by the clashing of cultural waves from east and west. It's in the air. And as Kenneth Clark said, Haga Sofia, which has been mosque and church and museum in its long life, is the world's most beautiful covered space.)

All of these things, yes, but I would also send you to Istanbul for its seafood sandwich. Fishing boats tie up on the west side of the Bosphorus, virtually under the shadows of the great mosques. The sea is green and seems always choppy, and these small veteran timber launches bob up and down on their moorings. Their motors are running; they sputter diesel fumes, and on the rear deck of each is a big basic wood-fired barbecue belching smoke and flames.

The crew operate an assembly line. One fillets silver, just-caught, mackerel-style fish. Another slices open buns. A third chops onions and cuts juicy green capsicums into batons. And the fourth, perhaps the captain, barbecues the fillets. There are lashings of olive oil and the perfume of the fish cooking and the oil burning competes with the diesel fumes. And the boats ceaselessly bob up and down.

Your challenge, if you choose to accept it, is to hold a finger up—meaning 'one'—and watch the crew assemble your sandwich. It will take perhaps four seconds. Fast food? But also sublime food. Is the fish fresh? Don't ask. It would be an insult. Then you've got to take your sandwich and pay for it, which is the tricky bit. (Remember that the boats bob.) It's an exchange, actually. One delicious, sublime fish sandwich wrapped in brown paper in return for a pittance. If you've won an Olympic relay gold, your experience at baton-changing will serve you well. The rest of us just do our best, and surprisingly few fish sandwiches are lost to the brine. Even less money is. And the sandwich is delicious. Don't encourage the seagulls.

Double-boiled milk and fish maw

Double-boiled milk is a favourite of Cantonese cooking. You'll see it listed regularly in the top restaurants of Hong Kong. Sometimes it's a savoury dish; at other times it's a dessert. It's versatile and popular. When I first came across it I imagined that the milk was subjected to two cooking procedures that might or might not have involved a complete or incomplete boil-up of the milk. (Is that enough of a glimpse into my mind?) In fact, double-boiling refers to the method of cooking the milk—in a receptacle of some sort over simmering water.

Cantonese cooking dictates that milk is double-boiled to enrich and thicken (slightly) it. But for no apparent chemical reason I know, it takes on a blinding whiteness as well. You almost need sunglasses to eat it (see 'Lady in pink').

On Hong Kong visits I'd seen double-boiled milk with various fishy bits listed in a host of restaurants. But it took a lot of courage to order it, which I eventually did, in one of the most reputable and esteemed of the region's eating places. And the dish I commissioned was double-boiled milk and fish maw. Dictionaries tell us that maw is craw, or related to the throats, lips, mouths or oral cavities of animals. But I discovered that fish maw is the swim bladders of fishes. At least, that's what I've been told, and I might very well be wrong. I'm certainly no anatomical expert. Fish maw, at any rate, is piscatorial—gristly and green when cooked.

Very expensive, it must be prepared for serving over at least a couple of days. Like a lot of seafood used in Chinese cooking, it is brought into the kitchen dried. I can imagine it looks like arid squiggles of seaweed or fungi about half a finger's length. It's soaked overnight then boiled for two hours. It's washed very carefully, rinsed, then soaked overnight and boiled a second time. The result is lengths of snot-green gristly slime, which is added to sweetened double-boiled milk to make a lovely pudding.

Disgusting? Yes, to look at, certainly, as a flotsam of turquoise maw drifts through the dazzling milk. But taste it, and there'll be an amazingly subtle and not at all revolting hint of the sea in the milk itself. And you can take or leave the slimy, gristly bladders. Food for Rambo eaters.

Roi's pickled roasted pork loin

Roi's Diner is in Victoria's exquisite Kiewa Valley, in which you could happily expire—after having eaten Roi's marvellous pork chop, certainly the world's best as far as I'm concerned. There are several great dishes of cooked pig, and this is one of them.

Roi Rigoni has been cooking professionally even longer than I've been writing about food, he jibes. So he has had an awful long time to perfect a dish that is both sublime and unprepossessing. Finding a great pig, killing and butchering it he leaves to a local butcher friend in Tawonga. To Roi's specifications, the butcher pickles its loins for two or three days in brine and pineapple juice, the proportions no doubt a secret. When Roi takes over, he scores its fat in parallel lines with a box cutter then rubs sea salt into the skin. Then he bakes it for a couple of hours in a moderate oven in what he specifies is a thin film of olive oil. He rests the loin for four hours before baking it a second time, basting it with house-made stock, in a hot oven for a further ninety minutes. After this, I suspect the meat-muscle is so relaxed it's virtually jelly. Roi, at any rate, believes it is only now worthy of final preparation for the plate.

At least a day elapses before the refrigerated and relaxed loin is served in the restaurant. When it's ordered, Roi slices off a chop from this already mighty construction, coats both sides with butter, seasons them and bakes the chop for fifteen minutes in a hot oven. And that's basically it, as far as the chop is concerned. But the garnishes are crucial.

They're sauerkraut—a good commercial one is fine—braised in the juice from the roasting tray, and mashed potatoes. But the brilliant tiara Roi's chop wears is what makes it so super-special, in my view. It's composed of arcs of Pink Lady apple (see 'Lady in pink'). Roi cores the apples, leaving on the skin, then slices them finely. The slices are fried in butter with white sugar and a drop or two of water. You melt the butter on a low heat. Once it bubbles, in go the apple slices to be cooked 'aggressively' to use Roi's word. Liquid evaporates, and you're left with translucent apple arcs of a stained-green colour you'll recognise from the *vitrails* of Europe's most splendid Gothic cathedrals. I can guarantee that your thoughts will turn spiritual, anyway, as you gobble down Roi's chop. It is wonderfully dense, lightly salty and very tasty. And when I last ate it, a strip of crackling accompanied that was so light and crisp it might have been pork meringue.

A Buenos Aires *parrilla*

Vegetarians should turn away, because this one is exclusively for carnivores. Argentinians eat more meat than the nationals of any other country. Their steakhouses—*parrillas*, or 'grills'—are not for the mealy of mouth. Even during the awful political problems of the late 1970s, they were full of life and eager eaters. My one and only visit to Argentina occurred during this time, and a lasting memory of the palpable fear ordinary Argentinians confronted daily runs parallel with indelible images of the *parrillas* I dined at.

They were impossible to miss. Whole carcasses of goats, sheep and pigs (I came to learn) were cooking in their front windows. There'd be a high, huge cone of red-hot coals around which the beasts barbecued, splayed on long metal pikestaffs stuck in at various angles to the radiant blast.

Then there were the braziers about the size of a couple of shoeboxes stacked one on top of the other. They sat on your table, and, presumably, the fire brigade parked outside. Entrée, as I recall, was composed of meaty bites of various and indefinite identities. (I have since understood that I might have eaten intestines, udder, lambs' testicles and sweetbreads in the Argentinian capital.) Most common are chicken and pork pieces, and lambs' kidneys. At any rate, the braziers contained a thick bed of coals and you cooked your meat to the degree you wanted on a grill perhaps half a hand-span above it.

An Argentinian *parrilla* is barbecueing in extremis (*see* 'Marinated lamb cutlets ...'), but unforgettable nonetheless. I have absolutely no recollection of what accompanied the meat—I think there might have been salads—or of what we drank as we ate. But I do remember that the steaks were sublime, the starter titbits sweet and of various intriguing and delicious tastes and textures. Argentina is a faraway destination for most people, but you really should drop by for the meat meal of your life. After it, you will yearn for no other.

Museo del Jamón

I can't stress how hard it is to eat better-than-average restaurant meals in Europe. Countries such as France and Spain and England need tougher critics who know food—reviewers prepared to shout, 'Hey, that emperor man there is starkers!' Only a few of the very best restaurants serve dishes that match in refinement and sophistication those of Australia's top eating places. And they are many times more expensive.

But I do recommend that you eat Spanish ham at one of the Museo del Jamón outlets in Madrid. And their slogan is right: they are the 'tastiest' museums in the Spanish capital. I looked recently for them in Andalusia— Seville and Granada. My quest failed, mainly because the company clearly has a marketing plan to conquer Madrid first.

I've been to two 'Museos', and they're a delight. They're simple, well-lit, bustling places where legs of ham of varying sorts and qualities hang around the dining rooms and the bars in scores. And if you visit the company's website, you'll see what trouble they go to in selecting pigs and making hams. The Museo del Jamón outlets offer a great deal more than ham, of course. You can order breakfast, sandwiches, combined plates, paella, tapas selections and several set menus. But I'd suggest you sample the prosciutto-style hams; they offer greater value for money and no-one has to cook anything. For a very reasonable sum you get a large plateful of slices accompanied by bread rolls. No butter. And when I asked why, I was told that they just didn't do it. And that was that. Order a tough little Spanish white to go with your ham and revel in the salty, sweet, dense textures and flavours of some of the world's greatest cured pig.

The most expensive ham is supposed to provide the best gastronomic experience. But experiment, and you'll come up with something that delights you at possibly a lesser sum.

La Luna's pasta marinara

Quiz an Italian and she'll own a traditional pasta marinara recipe, I'm told. It will differ from the one the women use in the village just down the road, but it will produce the only truly *authentic* pasta marinara. It might contain anchovies or whitebait, might even be enriched with cream or a velouté sauce, and it will almost certainly include tomatoes and herbs. But, more than likely, it will not be the multifaceted seafood pasta dish we have come to love in Australia. In Italy, our version of marinara would be considered excessive, exorbitant. (And it would be difficult to find the seafood.)

And that's mostly why I like what we do. Let me recommend the best that I know. It's served at La Luna Bistro in Melbourne, and it's great because it combines local seafood and fresh pasta (*see* 'Fresh homemade pasta'), one of the most exquisite combinations in gastro-heaven and now playing on Earth for an extended season.

La Luna's chef-owner Adrian Richardson goes to considerable lengths to maintain his dish's vivacity and consistency. He and his kitchen staff make fresh pasta from free-range eggs and plain flour every second day (at least) then hang the fettuccine—tagliatelle, pappardelle, call the strips what you like—on special racks for part-drying in the fridge. The miracle of fresh pasta is retained, says Adrian, by ensuring that the pasta ribbons are never *too* dry and will cook very quickly.

His marinara has two local seafood protagonists—they are not at all antagonistic, playing off each other as satisfyingly as two great voices in *The Pearl Fishers*' temple-depths duet. They're local blue mussels (*see* 'Steamed mussels') and calamari (*see* 'Fresh wokked calamari'). Adrian has a way of testing that the calamari he gets from reliable suppliers has been caught within the past twenty-four hours. He whacks it. If nerve-endings in the skin are still functioning, he says, the calamari briefly turns iridescent. And the mussels are firmly closed. Sometimes he adds large dice of fresh fish to the mix, and he makes his own half-dried roma tomatoes—an essential ingredient—on a rack above the stove.

When an order is called, olive oil, chopped garlic and chilli go in the pan. ('And don't be shy with it,' says Adrian.) When the edges of the garlic are turning golden, calamari—rings, wings and tentacles—are added. The mussels follow pretty quickly, and frying takes no more than a couple of minutes, sometimes with a lid over the pan to open stubborn bivalves. Meanwhile, a serving of pasta is thrown into simmering water and is done within the minute. Tomatoes and the pasta are added to the pan, and the last ingredient proper is a big handful of chopped flat-leaf parsley. Seasoning follows, of course, the key player being coarsely milled black pepper. 'It's all so simple,' says Adrian. I can think of another 's' word for it. Sublime.

Pho

First, an apology that the Vietnamese words among the next few hundred won't be decorated with the elegant accents of their correct calligraphy. The 'o' of the word 'pho' itself, for instance, is enhanced with a tiny question mark above it and a comma that joins it near the two o'clock position.

Pho is pronounced almost like 'fir'. It's the daily broth that sustains the morale, health and dignity of a nation whose history is characterized by invasion. Many nations have their soups, but no other potage or chowder, bouillon or consommé that I know of has had a conference organized in its honour. (No-one knows pho's precise derivation.) No other broth has been championed in books and pamphlets by a fine French cook, Didier Corlou, who is executive chef of the Sofitel Metropole Hanoi. His wife is Vietnamese and he is halfway through his second decade in Vietnam. Indeed, he has spent most of that time studying Vietnamese cooking and its peculiar combinations of wonderful fresh ingredients and spices. Spend a couple of hours with him and you will be convinced that pho is a work of genius. I am indebted to his research for much of the contents of this article.

Pho is usually a beef broth, but in some parts of Vietnam it is also made from a base of chicken, pork or fish bones, and/or meat. Sometimes it is simply a vegetable soup. But, beyond the stock, there are essential ingredients.

To die for

First and foremost are fresh rice noodles. Fried old ginger and shallots, which give brownness and flavour, are also mandatory. Then the spices: star anise, cinnamon, and what Didier Corlou calls 'black' cardamom. Finally, fresh flavour elements—the hallmark of Vietnamese cooking—are also essential: the juice of small dark-green lemons, spring onions, coriander and what Didier calls 'sweet' mint. (There are so many herbs in Vietnam. You will see dill and marjoram, for instance, as well as several sorts of mints. Each offers its own distinctive taste and the fresher the leaves the better.) Nuoc mam (which also has wonderful decorative accents when it's written properly) is the traditional Vietnamese sauce made from fish fermented in salt. Its delicate, salty and slightly rancid character seems to catalyze the best in other ingredients—and the mix itself. And, finally, rings of fresh chilli, which might be red, orange or green.

Didier Corlou calls pho—or rather the myriad versions of pho—the best soup in the world, surpassing even those of his native Brittany. Most Vietnamese eat it at least once a day, at any time of the day, but often at breakfast. In Hanoi, pho-eating is a huge part of the city's culture. It's a tonic and thousands of restaurants—many of them simply a simmering pot on the pavement, the additions scattered in bowls all around, the maker squatting by her broth—specialize in it.

Nguyen Dinh Rao, a gastronome in his seventies who is president of the UNESCO Club of Gastronomy in Hanoi, says pho originated in the early years of last century at Nam Dinh, an industrial city about eighty kilometres (fifty miles) south of the capital, to feed the workers, bureaucrats, and French and Vietnamese troops who were drawn there. He claims the 'mixed' population turned to its culinary roots to invent pho because they found local rustic concoctions such as a kind of rice gruel too substantial and less interesting. The original broth was built from beef bones and prawns; beef was added for Europeans, the noodles were local, and the finished assembly represented a kind of pan-Vietnamese as well as international culinary statement. The poet Vu Quan Phuong said that while pho might be international, its Vietnamese soul remained. He believed that pho 'makes up half of Vietnamese national pride; the second half is the popular war'.

While experts agree on its importance to the Vietnamese people, its name could come straight from French. The first pho sellers were street hawkers who strolled narrow alleys carrying a fire chest on one end of a yoke counterbalanced by pho ingredients at the other. '*Feu!*' they were alleged to have shouted, possibly as a safety precaution but also to advertize their soup. (Owing to the tonal ethnic language they spoke, their pronunciation could possibly have been more elongated than the snappy French exhortation '*feu*'. Hence 'fir', or 'fur' if you prefer.) Other sources say the origin of the name is in the Chinese character itself—whether cursive, classical or clerical is not detailed. Another source has it that pot-au-feu, the traditional French boiled beef with aromatic vegetables, inspired pho.

You get more elaborate and richer examples of pho in advanced countries such as Australia. And they're excellent. But you really should try pho in Hanoi, where it is the pie and sauce, the hamburger, the hot dog, the toad-in-the-hole, the daily life. The European Commission's office in the capital and the Sofitel Metropole have joined forces to list eighty purveyors of fine pho. There is a brochure with a map. Just pick one, decline to be squeamish, forget Western sanitary niceties, grab a low plastic chair or a shoe-high plastic stool and say 'pho'. Within minutes a bowl full of broth and its accompaniments will be in front of you. Didier Corlou details the ritual: squeeze on lemon juice, add chilli rings, then mix the soup with your chopsticks. Bring the bowl level with your mouth and get stuck into the noodles while drinking the bouillon with a ceramic spoon. (Metal spoons are not recommended 'because they are cold', he says.) You'll be consuming something absolutely delicious, but also understanding a culture a little bit better. You should despatch the noodles within five minutes because they swell and lose texture after that. Pay—usually a dollar or less—on your way out and take a toothpick.

There are excellent military, demographic and political reasons for Vietnam's success against the might of America. But those of us who have eaten pho on the streets of Hanoi know that Uncle Sam could have tried for a thousand years and never conquered the Vietnamese. I have an image of Charlie in his foxhole eating pho, strengthened by all it means. And another of a grim marine chewing on the best that the American food-processing industry could provide him—compressed concoctions packed with nutrition, triumphs of shelf-life and culinary compromise. Followed by a Hershey Bar.

Babka's Mongolian veal

Babka is the most brilliant café I know. Not only are the coffee and pastries superb, but Babka serves, until 6 p.m., bistro dishes that would be the envy of any restaurant in Melbourne.

Babka began as an independent bakery run by Sasha Lewis and her son Niko, who managed the ovens. But this tiny, modest place was soon compelled to offer more, simply because of its superb products. Consequently soups and 'wet' dishes—stews and braises and dumplings—were added to the list. And they took on a Russian leaning, only because Sasha's parents were Russian emigrants. Offerings such as borscht (beetroot soup) and pel'meni (lamb dumplings) are superb.

Choosing the best offering for you to sample before you expire, and you really must (taste it—oh, well, expire too one day but not soon, I hope), was ultimately pretty easy. It's the 'Mongolian' veal, so dubbed because Mongolia is halfway between Russia and China. It's a stupendous dish that demonstrates not just a political but also a gastronomic *rapprochement*.

For some time, Sasha and her chef Michael McGinlay had been poaching meat of various sorts in a Sino-influenced master stock containing soy sauce and palm sugar spiced with cinnamon, star anise and fennel seeds. They liked most the result they got with a basic cut of veal—blade, or shoulder. A sinewy part of the animal, it was rolled up and tied tightly then poached in the stock for anything up to a couple of hours. Rested, the meat had marvellous flavour and a melt-in-your-mouth texture.

Then Sasha noticed that when the stock was strained and cooled it turned into an exquisite amber jelly. (Veal throws heaps of gelatine as it cooks.) Why not serve big cubes of cold jelly with the veal? Michael thought a bland barley cake might absorb these flavours, and he set about creating one from grain, chicken stock, coriander leaf and spring onions. Dried and flattened discs of this 'porridge' are fried at the last minute in olive oil for serving.

And so the dish came about. You get four thick discs of wonderful veal wetted with the stock and warmed. They lean on a big wedge of barley cake, cubes of cold jelly accompanying in an adjacent birdbath. Longitudinally cut halves of roasted fennel complete the picture. Babka rotates its dishes quite a bit, so ring first to see when it's on next.

Sea cucumber and sharks' lips braised in carrot oil

This cartilaginous concoction by Cheong Liew (*see* 'Four dances of the sea') requires more time to prepare than any other dish in this book. I won't drag out the detail, suspecting almost all of you might choose not to knock up this little culinary number at home.

And Cheong is talking real sharks' lips and real sea cucumbers, the latter those bottom-dwelling animals that look a bit like a couple of hand-spans of fireman's hose. Cheong imports them dried from China; whole sea cucumbers come shrivelled to the size of barbecue snags. Many, many hours go into the initial preparation of these unusual delicacies, mainly in cleaning and rehydration. The lips are the easiest. They get soaked in water and simmered for several hours before Cheong and his team scrape off any remnants of sandpaper skin and shave away 'everything that is not cartilage'. Once that's done, the lips are cut into batons and simmered again in water containing salt, soy sauce, ginger, rice wine and spring onion for a further twenty-five to thirty minutes. Washing in cold water reinvigorates the lips, firming them up for final preparation.

Sea cucumber are scooped off the bottom of waters mainly around the islands to the north of Australia. Cheong says there are three general varieties: flat-bellied, those with nipples, and those with spikes. The nippled and spiked varieties are best, he says. But preparing them for the pot takes three days of repetitively burning and soaking and scraping them. Lime is used to produce dried varieties, and you must first burn it off with a naked flame. They're brushed and soaked and scraped time and time again, and when they're ready for a final simmer they're twice the size they were when dried. Again, they're simmered—Cheong calls it 'steaming'—in a mixture of water, soy, rice wine, ginger and spring onion. Cooked and cooled, they're cut into slightly larger batons than the pieces of lips.

Carrot oil is made by simmering a good neutral oil—peanut, grapeseed or sunflower, say—with grated carrot until the carrot flakes crisp up and float on the oil. The vegetable not only adds a brilliant orange-gold colour but also a beguiling sweetness.

And when the dish is called, the lips and sea cucumber batons are wok-fried in the oil with slices of carrot, bamboo shoots, shiitake mushrooms, vinegared chilli paste, a little sugar, soy sauce and rice wine, which is flamed. A small mount of oyster sauce, some spring onion lengths and crisp-fried leaves from the heart of the celery are added at the end.

And perhaps because it is such an exotic eat—the lips and cucumber are softly, slimily gelatinous and fairly bland in themselves—half-a-dozen seared scallops are added as well to firm up textures and add sweetness and flavour. The result, the times I've tried it, has been oily, spicy, sweet, jelly-like, complex, and completely and utterly wonderful. You might not like the sound of this dish, but once you've tasted it you'll despatch your serving with unexpected speed.

Peking duck

By 1985, when I visited, Beijing already had many restaurants specializing in peking duck. They looked like small drab factories. Grey, if I remember rightly, they were blockhouses that rose three or four storeys on frenetic street corners. And their names were often replete with irony; I recall the Sick Duck and the Blue Duck. You dined in them in groups, booking a large dim room with an enormous round table in the middle. Peanuts—and pickles, I seem to recall—began proceedings before you set upon the quackers reserved for your group. And I once read—probably in the very early years of China's throwing open its gates to foreign tourists—that one of these pek-duck factories had poisoned a busload of Germans, a few of them fatally. Authorities closed the place and several years passed before it was permitted to reopen.

Sino-tourism and the Chinese capital's signature dish have grown in popularity to such an extent these days that the obvious has happened: peking-duck chain restaurants now proliferate. The most popular is apparently Quan Jude, which trains its cooks and staff, grows its own ducks and makes its own secret sauce. It all sounds terribly capitalist in the world's biggest communist state. McDuck's more than McDonald's.

In Australia, scores of restaurants serve peking duck, and, in my experience, what they table is mostly pretty good. At the very least, you'll get several translucent small wheat pancakes into which you fold crispy-skinned slivers of duck flesh, batons of cucumber and spring onion and a tangy plum sauce. In posh places, you can pay a lot for a serving of just the pancakes. Paradoxically, in others you will be up for a fairly modest sum to take part in the whole gastro-theatre of peking duck. Old Kingdom in Melbourne is among the best of the latter, in my view. Eating peking duck in its fairly tatty surroundings (pink paper napkins, for instance, and stained and lifting wallpaper) is an experience simply TDF (to die for, you're right).

Owner Simon Lay asks for twenty-four hours' notice. (You can't just duck in. Couldn't resist.) Then his well-oiled duck-cooking gambit swings into action. A man of quiet humour, he says he relies on three poultry suppliers, one of them the Botanical Gardens! The ducks' cavities are filled with ginger, shallots, star anise and five-spice then sewn up. He pumps air in through the neck to separate the skin from the flesh. A dunking in very hot water follows, then a glaze of vinegar and malt extract is applied and the ducks are hung overnight. The next day, they're roasted and basted while they hang.

They come to the table whole, and Simon Lay delights in screwing off the heads and wings before paring thin slices with his deep Chinese cleaver. Their deeply tanned skin is paper-thin and brittle, protecting a layer of succulent fat covering tender, tasty flesh. Surf the Internet or rumble recipe books and you'll find many more complex variations on this basic theme—and probably all of them would result in very tasty tucker—but Old Kingdom value-adds. When enough skin-and-flesh slices are carved for a dozen or more pancakes, he takes the carcass away. The rest of the meat—quite a considerable amount—is removed and stir-fried with aromatic vegetables, bean shoots and spring onions, a second feast in itself. And some time after that comes the endgame, a rich clear broth containing tofu blocks, various greens and duck joints.

You're asked when you sit down your preference for steamed or fried rice, but you really don't need either. All by itself, OK's PK is a celestial repast. But, as

I've mentioned already, eat it first here—you could never be sure if it's going to be on up there. And, of course, some of us are more descenders than ascenders in the moral stakes.

Way Kee's oyster pancakes

If you can find this place you're doing well. But the reward is just exquisite—one of the world's great eats. Other basic cafés in Hong Kong do oyster pancakes, but Way Kee's are without peer.

Kowloon's famous Night Market is where it's at, not only for Way Kee's oyster pancakes. Here you'll also find bargain fob watches featuring Chairman Mao, who waves at you (and presumably a crowd somewhere) with each tick of the works. You'll reconnoitre a blinding array of gizmos and klipferdazzles, not to mention clothing, footwear, lights, knives and toys. And when the shopping has exhausted you, an oyster pancake is designed to pick you up.

Take a local with you, because I can't give you a number for Way Kee in Temple Street, just a vague direction that it's about halfway along on the western side. You'll see a narrow open eatery the looks of which are unlikely to spellbind you. Quite the contrary. Hang the hygiene! Brush past the batter and the wok brimming with boiling oil at the door and grab a wonky old stool at a worn laminex tabletop.

Way Kee's pancakes are made to order, and you'll see a ladleful of batter and perhaps a dozen oysters and a handful of spring onion lengths become a single pancake. The pancakes are at least as thick as a finger, crisp on the outside and halfway between liquid and solid within. The oysters they're plugged with are very tasty and have a light felty texture. A rich chilli sauce and fresh bouquets of coriander garnish.

To die for

Fenix's coconut noodles and chilli pork belly salad

There's a book on why Australian cooking is the world's most captivating and I've written it. Without reverting to the sort of detail I expounded in *Advanced Australian Fare*, let me just say that no other national culinary style has taken the idea of free cooking, which really began with the recognition of nouvelle cuisine in 1973, as far as Australia's has. For a variety of reasons, Australian chefs have become masters at using every and any appropriate ingredient and technique to create remarkable, original concoctions. They have pushed the envelope farthest, as the saying goes.

None more so than Raymond Capaldi, chef and part-owner of Fenix in Melbourne. His coconut noodles and chilli pork belly salad will become an Aussie classic, in my view. Now, Raymond very kindly talked me through its preparation. It took about twenty minutes, and if I tried to reproduce it in detail here I would make mistakes. So let me just present you with the gist of what he does.

The dish was inspired by a coconut–noodle offering in a restaurant called Thy Thy in Victoria Street, a big Vietnamese precinct. Raymond liked it so much he wanted to use it as a base for extra ingredients and what might politely be termed restaurant-style refinement. The entrée that arrives in front of you at Fenix, at any rate, is a central high cone of snowy white coils of noodles. They're cold, and buried in them and surrounding them are cubes of delicately spicy pork belly that are hot. On the plate is a smear of pale chilli oil and an absolutely brilliant sweet–sour emulsion 'haunted with characteristic laksa flavour', as I wrote when I reviewed the dish. Riding the noodles is the salad, which consists of coriander, Vietnamese mint, deep-fried shallots, sesame seeds, and shreds of green mango. Nut crumbs and squiggles of a dark-maroon fungi also featured in the version I tested.

Many separate procedures and a heap of work go into the creation. The pork belly—female, and therefore meatier and fattier than male bellies—is salted for three hours then washed and dried and roasted in its own fat with sweet chilli sauce, palm sugar, chilli and garlic. The noodles are made from a blend of fresh and canned coconut milk, chilli oil and palm sugar. Powdered Japanese agar-agar extracted from red seaweed is stirred into the mix, which sets into shallow and lightly gelatinous white lakes. These are passed through the wires of an Italian chitarra, which looks something like a guitar, to create the square laces. Fish sauce, two sorts of vinegar and pineapple juice are also players in this marvellous triumph of stovework. And once it's assembled, you should do what Jacques Derrida never had the chance to do with it because in France or the United States it would never have featured on restaurants lists. You deconstruct it. Don't miss it!

Cha ca at La Vong

My apologies are renewed about the wonderful accents above, below and near many of the letters in Vietnamese words (*see* 'Pho'). *Cha ca*—or *ca qua* or *ca lang*—is a ricefield catfish also nicknamed banana fish or snake fish because of its elongated shape and skin. La Vong was a single tiny restaurant in the old quarter of Hanoi until its huge popularity allowed it to open a sister place in the capital and a third outlet in Ho Chi Minh City. It serves only one dish—fried *cha ca*—but there is so much theatre attached to it and so many accompaniments that it's worth the slight detour to Vietnam from wherever you're living just to eat it.

Terracotta braziers brimming with red-hot coals on restaurant tables? In most of the developed world's eating places it wouldn't be on. Fire and indemnity insurance would cost prohibitively. But braziers are on the tables at La Vong, of course, and they're central to this classic dish.

You sit down, and about ten minutes later out comes a copious amount of rice noodles and vegetable accompaniments in many bowls. They're scattered around your table, followed by the brazier, which has the diameter of, say, a small dinner plate. It's placed centrally. And, finally, a waiter carries in a thin and battered long-handled aluminium saucepan. In it sizzles a deep pool of vegetable oil and yellow-stained cubes of fish. (They're rolled in turmeric.) The pan goes on the brazier, of course, the oil continuing to bubble, the fish to cook.

The platefuls that follow have many nuances, depending on how you mix and match the ingredients with the fish in the pan. You have a lot to choose from. There are roasted peanuts, rings of a fiery orange chilli, a huge bowl of dark-green sprigs of dill and logs of spring onion, brilliantly fresh branchlets of dark marjoram and coriander, shavings of the white and bulbous root-ends of another type of young onion, a bowl of nuoc mam (fish sauce) and, of course, the massive mound of noodles. The waiter who brings the pan leads off; he or she takes serving chopsticks and prongs a considerable quantity of dill and dark spring onions into the pan and stirs. Rice noodles will be served into your (empty) eating bowl, and, after a minute or so, the fish, onions and dill will follow. Peanuts will be strewn on top, then, through gestures, your waiter will convey the message that you should start eating, adding what pleases you of the other ingredients.

The fish cubes themselves are firm and lightly flavoured, haunted by turmeric. Didier Corlou (*see* 'Pho') says that other lesser species these days are being substituted for *cha ca*, even in the La Vong stable of restaurants. Be that as it may, the supreme quality of the ingredients overall suggests to me that whatever fish La Vong uses must be excellent—it certainly tastes that way. And the whole theatre of the dish is utterly beguiling.

— · —

Eating in

Home-cooked cray

The myth goes that crayfish—or southern rock lobster, as the industry would prefer me to call it—was eaten as often as boiled eggs in the Australia of the 1950s. I don't think so! But it is true that it was somewhat less expensive, relatively speaking, than it is these days. Asian markets were not yet elevating its price, not yet demanding it in vast quantities. And every so often, and that meant at least once a year when I grew up, many households would eat cray with mayonnaise. Even in wowserish Protestant homes, the sweet, snowy flesh of Australia's most popular crustacean was occasionally permitted. (Sex wasn't, as writer Tom Keneally, of Catholic background, points out, because it might have led to dancing.)

Part of the culture said your cray had to be boiled in a kerosene tin. A clear blue liquid petroleum, kerosene fuelled extremely smelly and dangerous heaters in those days. It was sold in rectangular tin-plated drums. You got out the tinsnips, cut around the top, gave the drum a bit of a rinse and there was your cray cooker.

I saw it done—in a rented backyard in coastal Point Lonsdale in the mid-1950s. But back then, Australia still hadn't got gastronomy, and I seem to recall that the poor animal, its tail convulsing rhythmically, was thrown into boiling salted water alive. I remember a loud sigh, a thrash, and sloughed legs floating to a foamy surface. Eating is a brutal business. It was school holidays, and the men stood around the campfire, the kero tin and the cray, smoking. (Perhaps some of them weren't Methodists and gripped beers.) And perhaps half an hour later, the cray was brought into the house and allowed to cool. And another hour after that we sat around the laminex tabletop, in a glaring-yellow faux semiprecious stone, and consumed the cray. Apart from salt and pepper, only bottled mayonnaise went with it.

To die for

My mother showed me how to break a cray leg gently so that a long worm of softly gelatinous flesh could be withdrawn. You competed with other family members to expose the longest, barest and most perfect leg. (Yes, yes! It all came back when I first saw the Lido girls in Paris; these 'madeleines' not far from La Madeleine reminded me of crayfish.) The sweetness and soft jelly-like texture of that first leg are unforgettable. An introduction to sensuality, this process aroused me then and stood me in good stead when I later began ripping off tights. Female persons', that is.

Because of its cost these days, live cray remains a very infrequent delicacy in most Australian homes. I stopped buying them, even annually, by the early 1990s. But we should all hoard our pennies and do it occasionally. Buy it live, please, but be kind to your cray. Some chefs still insist on bisecting them wholly conscious. More humane ones put them to sleep for an hour or so in the freezer. I've never liked smashing them between the eyes with a cleaver, nor felt really comfortable drowning them in a large pot, a brick on the lid. But if you feel up to it, do it. (They say severing the spinal cord is the best way to go. Call in your local neurosurgeon.)

Once dead, your cray should be simmered with lots of fresh herbs from the garden, parsley stalks making a grand contribution, and a little white wine. Be careful with seasoning. Don't overcook your cray—even a big cray shouldn't be simmered for more than half an hour. And please make your own mayonnaise (see 'A proper mayonnaise').

Southern rock lobster has such a sweet, cloying flavour that it dominates any other foodstuff. Eat it just with salt and pepper if you don't like mayonnaise or a well-made vinaigrette (see 'A proper vinaigrette'). And drink a big white wine—chardonnay is the best, in my view—with it.

Old-style thermidor and mornay sauces are far too rich and creamy to go with an already powerful protagonist, while, as sashimi, cray is a rank disappointment. (Cold and raw, its virtually transparent tail flesh is almost without flavour, its sweetness absent.) Grilling dries it and leads to famous cases that restaurant critics sometimes lose to juries.

And it's a cray or crayfish, despite what authorities want us to call it. Lobsters have big spanner-like claws in front. Crays don't.

Marinated lamb cutlets cooked over a real barbecue

First choose your lamb. If you're squeamish, you won't want to go for what were called 'milk-fed beasts' that are only weeks old, tiny and have never chewed on even a single blade of grass. They were terribly in vogue about a decade ago, but perhaps our sensibilities have improved; I haven't seen them on restaurant lists for ages.

But do select small cutlets. The flesh should be tightly textured and appear smooth. Its colour should be pale and halfway between pink and fawn. Make your own marinade, of course, but I'd suggest a basis of olive oil and a dash of red wine vinegar. Season it well with salt and coarsely ground black pepper— ready-ground white pepper is too abrasive and not aromatic enough. And from there you do your own thing. You might like to add crushed chopped garlic, fresh herbs from the garden. Rosemary, which is usually too strong to use in most cooking, may be added to a marinade like this one. It complements sheep meat well. How long you marinate your meat is up to you. To get any effect at all you should count on a minimum of at least three to four hours.

Now, the barbecue. And, more particularly, why I specify a real one. You see, the word, the concept, the culinary idea has been terribly corrupted by money and marketing to the extent that most people who think they own a barbecue actually possess a small coffin on wheels, the principal purpose of which is to flout key culinary principles. I'm talking about two main ways in which heat is conveyed to food: frying and radiation. A gas barbecue with a hotplate, which most people seem to prefer, allows you to fry food but not at the temperatures required to seal in the juices. You get seepage from the meat being cooked, and a subsequent loss of succulence and flavour. Equally, a gas barbecue with an iron grill-grate lets you cook using heat radiated from the burners. But, again, we're talking low temperatures and not the red-hot blasts you need to crisp immediately the outside surfaces of meat to padlock its qualities.

Modern barbecues, which look flash, I'll agree, simply don't do the job. They're sold by the unethical to the gastronomically uneducated. And the lazy, of course. None of us wants to get out the axe to chop wood. Let alone buy it. But a barbecue *is* cooking over an open fire. It *must* be that to get the best results. So beg, borrow or steal your wood. I've never been short of it on a suburban block due to building extensions over many years, fence replacements, and native trees shedding branches and needing pruning. And until big companies took over the production and sale of this Aussie icon, backyards and parks were littered with the real thing—thin steel bars over open fires. It stood to reason.

Barbecuing is cooking by heat radiated from red-hot to white-hot coals. Its origin is supposedly among the dreaded Carib cannibals of the Caribbean, who devised a *barbacoa* (the Spanish version of their word). It was a grate of green wood on which strips of meat were draped to cook or to dry. *Encyclopaedia Britannica* says the fire was 'slow'. And one reference I consulted displays the inevitable fine etching of human limbs rotating on a kind of spit near a warrior wearing no more than a fantastic headdress. He carries an enormous club, and a tribeswoman approaches him carrying a nice bit of human hindquarter. 'Here, dear,' she's probably saying, 'the kids are coming tonight as well.'

The *Compact Oxford English Dictionary* cites barbecue's origins as Haitian or Guyanan and quotes Dampier's referring, in 1697, to sleeping on a *borbecu* or platform of sticks supported by posts about a metre off the ground. Presumably, he was one of the lucky ones who beat the cooks out of bed. The

OED also describes as an 'absurd conjecture' the notion that barbecue comes from the French *barbe queue,* or cooking from head to tail.

Many food books ignore barbecuing altogether. Some will refer to grilling over hot coals in a chimney. And even more will note that restaurant grilling is achieved over rocks or pseudo-rocks of some sort heated by gas. So real barbecuing is not only fun, but it's a wonderful, atavistic way of producing food. And you have good control over its heat.

First, build a roaring fire. Use hardwoods—red gum is excellent—but don't be tempted by timber that has been steeped in preservatives or painted; there's a chance it's deadly. You're going to cook over the red-hot coals after the fire dies down, not the flames. You might actually still have an old-fashioned barbecue on wheels, which is much more convenient than bending over a ground-level fire to cook. Wait for your flames to die, leaving a mattress of coals as thick as a clenched fist. You won't get enough heat otherwise. Using a stout bit of wood or a barbecue tool, rake flat the surface of your embers. Next comes the grill over the top. Make sure your bars are thin, allowing maximum heat radiation. About half a hand-span should separate them from the coals. Then barbecue.

How long you cook your chops depends on their thickness and how you want your meat to come out. Thin cutlets take only a minute or so. Flames will engulf them when the oil from the marinade drips on to the coals. Char them a little but don't burn them. And cook the reverse side only about half as long as the first. Flavour is imparted by the gases and solids emanating from the coals, and sugar is gained in caramelizing the fat and protein of the meat. You can experiment with flavours by burning vine clippings, say, as they do in France, over the coals. I often put fresh rosemary branches between the grill-bars and the meat. The results are always magnificent. Death to gas barbecues!

To die for

Properly cooked chips

Good chips—French fries, if you prefer the Americanism—are scarce in homes or restaurants. Why? Because commercial kitchens and home cooks apparently have better things to do than adhere to the simple but time-consuming and rigorous process that produces them. But for the home cook, at least, such an explanation is a feeble excuse. We've got plenty of time to respect food and enjoy eating to its zenith. We should be able to produce routinely the perfect chip. Always.

If I were to put a figure on it, perhaps a third of all chips I'm served in restaurants are perfect. There are no excuses for less than the best, but explanations might be that chefs are trying to produce chips from the wrong potatoes or they're buying them ready-cut instead of starting from scratch. They might be deep-frying them in stale oil or at too low a temperature because of a fear of setting the kitchen alight. But all this says is that they're not making the effort needed to cook chips properly.

It was quite an epiphany for me to be taught how to do it well. My French in-laws have tutored me brilliantly in food and cooking—as you'll see from other items in these pages. This time, a brother-in-law took me aside. He showed me that to get a proper chip you've got to cook it twice. As simple as that. Well, not quite.

What is the perfect chip? Well, size doesn't count all that much. I've eaten sublime chips in matchstick dimensions and quite large, gnarled ones that were terrible. Characteristics, though, *do* count. Chips' surfaces should be tanned to a mid-golden-brown and be very crisp, as brittle as a boiled lolly and parchment thin. So crisp, indeed, that you should be able to snap the chip like dry kindling. Inside, the cooked potato will be soft and cloudy. If the chip is good enough you should be able to blow away, almost, this potato-fluff.

Recently, I did some trials. I bought pink-skinned desirées, waxy kipflers and flimsy-skinned new potatoes. Shop around, and at least one cookery expert will tell you each has the best attributes to make chips. I seem to remember having been told that the wateriest potatoes make the best chips. Perhaps. In my case, the new potatoes were the wettest after peeling, kipfler the driest and desirée somewhere in-between. I cut my chips to about the size you see in fish and chip shops and dried their surfaces well in a tea towel.

Now, a fresh frying medium is important, but you can get away with using some fats a couple of times. What you can't get away with is using an electric deep-fryer as it's simply not possible to get the fat hot enough. Instead, use a metal tub of simmering fat placed over a flat-out wok-burner, if you've got one, or the strongest burner on your stove. Into this tub you will lower your wire basket containing your chips. First, heat the fat so that the surface of the oil begins to smoke. This will take several minutes, during which you might like to get out the fire brigade's number. The fryer should be only about half full. Be very careful! If the fat goes into the fire the result is pretty certain to be tragic. Equally, if your chips are wet and they contact fat of this temperature you could have an explosion and yet another holocaust—it's why you dry the surfaces of chips *before* you fry them. (My wife's Tante Luisette suffered extensive burns quite recently cooking chips. The *pompiers* were called. We, the family, feel she shouldn't be deep-frying at ninety-four.)

Don't put too many chips in the immersion basket. Three or four handfuls is an adequate amount, and if it takes you several loads to cook your chips that's life. Now, when the fat is at smoke-point and your uncooked chips are in the basket, lower the basket *gently* into the fat. There'll be a grand commotion and lots of bubbling. *Don't be afraid* to withdraw the basket partially if the fat looks as if it's going to bubble over the edge of the fryer into the fire. Once in and settled, the bubbling lessens considerably. Leave the chips to cook for a good ten minutes, vigorously shaking the basket every so often. When one or two of your chips are tanning at this halfway stage and floating to the surface of the fat, take out the whole basket and empty your chips onto kitchen paper to drain. Continue with more portions.

What you've done, of course, is a first frying, which should essentially cook the chips, not imbue them with the tanned crispy crust and blow-away interior they'll eventually acquire. That comes next.

Having cooked all your chips a first time, wait again for your oil to begin to smoke. This time, it's an advantage to have even fewer chips in your basket. So put in two or three handfuls, watch for the smoke, then plunge in the basket. You'll see a lot less bubbling, and there will be almost no danger of overspills. Rattle the basket as vigorously as you like to separate the chips and ensure that they share equally the temperatures throughout the oil. Don't be so vigorous, of course, as to upset your deep-fryer together with its contents onto your Italian tiles. Or, God forbid, the burner! And when the chips are tanned, they'll be done. It will take only a minute or so before it's time to remove, drain and eat. Then pine forever in restaurants and private homes when you get served less than the best.

I liked the results all three varieties of potatoes gave me, by the way. If anything, the kipfler had a little more interior density and flavour.

Asparagus with a vinaigrette

As a French child, my wife hid in the asparagus. Her father's asparagus that is, and she took refuge when there were chores to be done, she admits, rather sheepishly, these days. That there was enough asparagus (it had obviously run to seed) in which to hide in a post-war provincial French garden indicates the importance it had then as an entrée. It still does. Moreover, in French homes it's always served with a vinaigrette sauce (*see* 'A proper vinaigrette').

Growing up at the same time half the world away, I thought asparagus came from a can. As uniform as sardines, the spears were an insipid green the colour of roof lichen and more fragile than the Dead Sea scrolls. Flaccid? Intravenous Viagra wouldn't have helped them. And about the only way they were eaten was wrapped in thin slices from a white bread sandwich loaf. Pride of place, they took, at such gastronomic events as Anglican fetes and school bazaars. Toothpicks held them together.

Nowadays, of course, asparagus is a popular vegetable in homes and restaurants. You'll get it as a garnish—fanned across the plate under seafood, say, or bundled like a peasant's kindling next to a fillet of beef. Domestic cooks tend to add asparagus spears to salads. Well, all that is fine, but there's only one way to eat asparagus, in my view, and that's the French way. So set are the Gauls in their habits, that from my mother-in-law's estate we acquired a wonderful high-sided piece of porcelain decorated with five asparagus spears in bas-relief on the bottom. Each end of the dish is cupped to form reservoirs for cooking juice draining from the spears. And, curiously enough, the plate is also decorated with vine leaves, hinting at the red wine vinegar with which you should produce your sauce.

When you cook asparagus at home you should cut through the spears just above their woodiness—you can feel the right point through the knife. Stand them in an asparagus cooker if you've got one or tie them in a bundle and stand them in an ordinary pot. Boiling water should come about two-thirds of the way up them and a lid balanced on top helps the steaming process. Don't undercook asparagus. They will take a lot longer than the nonsensical times some so-called cooks delight in. Ten minutes, actually, is not too long. The bottom half of each spear should be soft, the top half graduating to light crunchiness at the tips. You forgo flavour by giving them less heat.

There are several varieties of asparagus, and white asparagus is produced from one of them, it goes without saying. But it's still only asparagus; it just hasn't been allowed to sprout above the soil, see the light of day and turn green to photosynthesize. White has a milder but very seductive flavour and is enhanced with sauces based on strong nut oils such as those pressed from walnuts and hazelnuts.

My plum jam

Now, no queue-jumping here! I'm being very unfair, yes, I know. But it's a good bet that almost all of you will unfortunately never get the chance even to taste my plum jam let alone steal a jar of it. But it's certainly one of the last things I'd like in my mouth before I slide away to oblivion. (That's my idea—you might have others equally legitimate.)

The fruit for my jam comes from a solitary tree. In good years, I'll make forty to fifty jars from it. (And, of course, harvest a lot of fruit for eating fresh.) In almost three decades of owning this particular tree, I've been unable to say precisely what variety of plum it is. The fruit are of medium size, their skin a dark plum colour (funny, that) when they're fully ripe. Inside, the flesh is much paler—from a stained-glass red to a pale yellow-orange, depending on maturity. They're very juicy fruit, increasingly so as they mature. An old edition (1942) of _The Australian Gardener_ by Leslie H. Brunning says plum trees can grow to a great age, and I suspect that my tree is as old as the subdivision where I live, or about eighty years. The _Gardener_ lists forty-two varieties of plums that must have been common in Australian backyards in the 1940s. Is mine a red heart or a ballena, a hermosillo, siler, robe de sargeant or early orleans? No-one knows.

As I write, I can see it through the window. From a very thick trunk it straggles several metres into the air in all directions. In a few weeks it will burst into blossom, but its bare skeleton shows numerous infirmities, large holes weeping a kind of purulent sawdust, parasitic lichens and broken branches. I never prune it nor give it fertilizer. Perhaps I am neglectful in the extreme and uncaring of another living thing. But every year almost without fail it bears the most beautiful fruit. (I say 'almost' because storms at the wrong time have occasionally decimated the crop, and for inexplicable reasons its yield is very occasionally low.)

But most years I simply go out with a rickety ladder on or about 31 December, pick fruit and make jam. I will usually do it three times. My modus operandi for jam-making with this fruit is simple. Equal weights of jam and white sugar; cut the plums up roughly, always retaining the pips; boil, and test on a cold white plate. When the jam is a brilliant red and just thickening after a minute or so on the plate, stop the cooking and bottle. There is considerable margin for error. I've tried adding other things such as citrus rind or more sugar, but the best jam is only and ever equal weights of fruit and sugar. It's sweet and tart and firm and succulent and fruity and tasty and wrings your salivary glands ... It's just heavenly. But get in before the Man upstairs does.

A proper vinaigrette

I was all alone—as many of us are—on my first night in Paris. (Life shouldn't be like that, but it means things can only improve.) I'd booked into a cramped and ancient little two-star hotel on the Left Bank called the Pierwige. It was after eight by the time I settled into my fifth-floor room (no lift) and seen the drugged girls in their underwear through a half-ajar door from the tiny landing of the fourth. I'd bucked across the Channel on that brilliant British invention, the hovercraft, and taken a slow-moving train from Boulogne. I simply wanted to eat something, get excited by the smells and the noise of the city then collapse into bed, with or without the drugged girls from the floor below.

To die for

Across the street from my hotel was a maroon-canopied Parisian café. I went in, made myself understood enough to order steak and chips—what else would an Australian order until he comprehended that it's the French national dish as well?—and a carafe of bad red wine. At the next table, a short, shrivelled man with grey hair and a severe countenance wiped his plate clean with bread. Using a fork and spoon, he took salad greens from a medium-sized bowl in front of him, warehousing them on the now-pristine porcelain. He added salt, pepper, vinegar and oil to the bowl from various small receptacles on the table. After whisking these together with the spoon, he returned the leaves to the bowl and folded the lot over several times. I smiled at him. He flickered a grin.

My steak and wine materialized. Mustard in a small ceramic pot, and a pressed-metal basket of chips also arrived. I recognized the cut of beef. We called it 'skirt steak' in Australia. It was the lowest form of muscle. My mother minced it for cornish pasties, which was her only gastronomic flourish, if you could call it that. But French skirt steak was surprisingly good. The chips were crisp, their innards of cloudy, blow-away lightness. And what was it about French potatoes that gave them so much flavour?

My green salad appeared, and I shook salt and pepper onto the leaves. The shrivelled diner at the next table frowned. I picked up the oil and was about to add it when he gestured frantically. '*Ah, non, monsieur!*' His grin had disappeared altogether. His shaking head dictated that I put down the oil.

'*Faites l'espace,*' he said, which was beyond my comprehension. He made a clearing motion with his hand. I picked up the spoon and began toying with the leaves. He gestured again. I cleared some to one side. He grinned. I pushed all the leaves to the edge of the bowl. He was delighted. I picked up the oil again. His grin disappeared.

'*Ah, non, monsieur! D'abord, le sel et le poivre.*' I must have looked mystified; he picked up his own salt and pepper. I sprinkled seasoning into the bowl, even if I'd done it over the leaves already. We smiled at one other. I picked up the oil. His hand shot out, hooking my elbow.

'*Pas encore, monsieur!*' I replaced the oil. '*En premier, le vinaigre.*'

Vinaigre? Had to be. I picked up the vinegar. My instructor smiled. '*Pas trop,*' he insisted. As this was accompanied by a fingertip and thumb only fractionally apart, I guessed he meant that I shouldn't add too much. I poured and replaced, then picked up the oil.

'*Bien!*' he said.

I poured and stirred. He smiled. I pulled back the leaves over the sauce and tossed them. A fulfilled pedagogue, the man held his arms aloft like a heavyweight champion.

Later, my many sisters-in-law gave me more formal instruction in making a proper vinaigrette. Seasoning at the bottom of the bowl; vinegar in first to give the salt the best chance of dissolving; then oil, about three parts oil to one part vinegar. And that's a proper vinaigrette, and if you do it every time you make a salad—don't make it in advance to keep in the refrigerator, you can tell the difference—you will be richly rewarded. You can complement a vinaigrette with mustards of various sorts and choppings of herbs. The owner-chefs of some top eating places leave vinaigrettes unemulsified, a terribly fashionable affectation. My argument is that if you put things in a bowl to be conjoined then you ought to bloody well conjoin them. But then, most of us agree that the emperor's new clothes hang just so.

A proper mayonnaise

I learned to make proper mayonnaise watching my late French mother-in-law. A woman who could look exceptionally attractive when she tried, she was at her ugliest making mayonnaise. Her face contorted into a kind of grimace of the damned, the rictus of a Goya subject, brought on by fear that her mayonnaise would not emulsify properly, not rise by many times its volume into this sublime thick creamy cloud of oil and egg yolk it should become—by rights and for technical reasons.

Mayonnaise is magic. Every home cook should learn to conjure it. In my childhood it was unthinkable that many foodstuffs could ever be made at home. Spaghetti was thin, short worms in a kind of canned tomato soup. Sardines could never have swum, must have been some headless, artificial representation of a fish that was bought in tins. And until I lived in France, I'd always presumed mayonnaise was the generic name for a cold jelly turned out of jars. In fact, preparing it is one of the best reasons for cooking. And I'm convinced that my mother-in-law actually quite enjoyed the ritual of making it, so close was it to a kind of culinary death-denial, a bungee-jump by the sink.

You see, no-one really understands what exactly happens when you make mayonnaise. Technically speaking, it's a temperate emulsion of egg yolk and oil. But that's only technically speaking. Beyond the universe of physical chemistry are realms you and I may only dream of. I could cite scientific articles that prove this, but scientists scarcely write entertaining prose.

The ingredients for mayonnaise should not be cold! Indeed, the canny cook places her egg and oil side-by-side on a kitchen bench half an hour before the operation so that they have equivalent temperatures—something near that of the room. She also sees that the egg and the oil are fresh, although some people will swear that they get more consistent results with staler makings.

To make a mayonnaise you break an egg yolk into a bowl then whisk oil into it. Simple! But the process must go slowly. You begin with only a few drops of oil, progressing to a thread then finally a thin stream. This might take about ten minutes. You know very quickly—at thread stage—if your mayonnaise is emulsifying properly; by then it should be opaque, have a light jelly-like texture and a volume considerably more than its separate components.

In households where I first saw mayonnaise produced, nothing more nor less than a table fork was used for the whisking. Whisks themselves were absent, as were those special mayonnaise-making implements that look something like a flat spoon with a narrow rim of coiled wire. And I can't imagine any mechanical blender could constantly aerate the whole bulk of the mixture as you must do when you make mayonnaise.

In its heyday during the late 1980s, the Burdekin Hotel dining room in Darlinghurst had a terrific party trick: using forks, the serving staff would make mayonnaise at your table. During a busy service, supple wristwork and the oil-flow judgement of a Texas billionaire were needed.

Because of the technical fragility of mayonnaise, a certain amount of folklore attends its preparation in France. It's believed that you can't succeed unless beating is continuous—prolonged rapid thrashing. Secondly, any gust of wind, breeze, draught or even expelled breath can split your sauce and turn it runny. Consequently, many home cooks take a large breath and hold it for the entire procedure. Since seeing that, I've understood why France has been a pioneer in free diving, especially women's events. Strangely, I've never seen many bung RSI wrists strapped to plastic moulds in France.

You season your mayonnaise, of course, and can add lemon juice or vinegar to cut all that fat. Even water, which makes it whiter and lighter. You can also add herbs and tomato paste to make various versions of one of the greatest of Gallic classics.

A proper hollandaise sauce

This sauce and its sister béarnaise are what are technically called hot emulsified concoctions. But not too hot! If you cook them too much, the protein in them will flocculate into tiny squiggles and the fat will become clear. Your sauce will 'split', as they say in professional kitchens. But if you go easy, there's no reason why you can't make a sublime hollandaise or béarnaise.

What emulsifies is cold butter and egg yolk. A natural flavouring makes the sauce. In the case of hollandaise, the flavouring is lemon juice—and seasoning, of course. For béarnaise, it's a concentrated extract of shallots, good vinegar and lots of tarragon. (Some recipes add garlic as well.) You should experiment with the quantities involved. You don't need much vinegar—perhaps only a thin layer in the bottom of a small saucepan—and a large shallot chopped and crushed usually does the trick. Boil these ingredients then strain your reduction, pressing the shallots well. Let it cool. The amount you finally extract should be no more than enough to coat the bottom of a heavy-bottomed saucepan.

But the guts of the matter is the yolk and butter emulsification. Basically, you put one or two egg yolks in your saucepan with the flavouring and whiz them around for a few seconds with a wooden spoon. Then over low heat or a double boiler (bain-marie) you add cubes of cold butter from the fridge, letting one melt before you add the next—or near enough to melting. Your sauce will thicken magically. This is one of the great moments in the culinary arts. You'll see a gelatinous texture appear from nowhere. When it does, and your sauce is hot to taste, it's ready. Take it off the heat! Don't proceed further, attempting to get a stiffer gelatinous texture. You'll find that even off the heat the sauce will continue to thicken. It will be marvellous, and you will be so proud of yourself for making one of the giant confections of French cooking. Add seasoning, check it and serve. Recipes will vary in the amount of butter they tell you to add. For each yolk you can count on adding roughly as much butter as will mound up in the palm of your hand. And you'd cut it into about five separate bits to add to the egg yolk. One yolk's worth makes enough hollandaise or béarnaise easily to serve two. But always have more than enough butter. And make sure it's the best quality you can get.

Steamed mussels

I returned to Australia something of a gastro-zealot after having lived in France. I suppose, looking back, it was natural. But it should not have resulted in the sort of behaviour that is these days actually and justly criminal. If no-one was harvesting the wonderful mussels in Port Phillip Bay, I reasoned in the mid-1970s, why shouldn't I? It was food—wonderful, glorious food of exceptionally high quality. You'd pay a fortune for it in France. So my wife and I would go to the beach of a Sunday afternoon, enjoy the sun like true wogs, then fill a bucket or two with fresh mussels, straight off the rocks. (To my shame, we once took seventeen dozen of various sizes—I counted them.) We got strange looks. But what onlookers made of my Irish-ocker caste and my wife's blonde northern-European physiognomy is anyone's guess.

Within a few years, though, significant numbers of Asian immigrants had arrived and—with Europeans already harvesting them—terrific pressure was put on the natural Port Phillip Bay mussel population. Inevitably, collecting mussels was banned. Mind you, none of us, even the poorest of Asian immigrants, really needed to pinch them. Farmed mussels remain of high quality and are very competitively priced. Moreover, the magnificent blue mussel (*Mytilus edulis*) is harvested year-round in the bay and around the Tasmanian coast. I hope you can get your hands on them where you live.

Mussels were bait when I was a child, and some people still have funny ideas about them. Some say the best are supposed to be the smallest, which is idiotic. Small mussels mean a small animal that can become wizened and leathery in cooking. Even the biggest of these shellfish cooked just until they open can have the most exquisite lightly gelatinized flesh.

Clean mussels by pulling out the beard and roughly scraping off any weed or seagrass attached to the shell. Rinse them quickly under running water.

Retain only mussels that are firmly closed or snap shut pretty promptly when you begin to interfere with them. (Just like a chaste young lady.)

Cooking them is easy. Put them in a lidded pot with crushed and chopped garlic and lots of fresh herbs from the garden—long stalks of parsley gone to seed, rocket from the back lawn, a couple of bay leaves and marjoram, say—lemon grass and fresh chilli. Use your imagination, they're your mussels. Add a trickle of good olive oil and a three-second glug of white wine. No other liquid should be added, it must be stressed. And be careful with the wine; restaurants often add too much, a vinous flavour overwhelming the bivalves' delicacy. Unwooded whites are best.

Put the pot on full blast, lid on, and in a matter of minutes your mussels should split open, spilling their juices. Stir them occasionally to even up the heat. In a few minutes they'll be ready for eating. Remove the pot from the flame immediately most of the mussels have opened. (Toughies can be prised open with a little attitude and a knife.) Boil down somewhat the cooking juice, which might be salty because it consists mainly of the liquids the mussels have lived in. But have confidence; flavour should, in the end, override the salt. Add a big blob of cream and serve.

A great brown sauce

Now, why should I suggest that you make the king of classical sauces, a concoction so outmoded and rich these days that you rarely see it even in restaurants? For the same reason that I think you ought to listen, at least once in your life, to a late Beethoven string quartet or Bach's *Goldberg Variations*. These things are the best in their fields, sublime, the greatest of human expressions, exemplars of the zenith that humankind can attain, and you ought not to expire without trying them.

Moreover, you can revel in all these things at home. Even the sauce. I'm not talking about your making an *approximation* of a great brown sauce. I'm talking about your producing the real thing, the precise, great culinary monster. You *can* do it and do it easily. And as you sup on it you can imagine all the most esteemed and wealthy people in all the most lavish dining rooms and palaces the world has seen—the kings and the queens, the dukes and the designates—and realize that they ate this and *precisely* this precious liquid under their tournedos rossini and rosbifs a hundred years ago. Neat thought, I think. You can tell your friends you have actually, truly eaten like European aristocracy in the *belle époque*. (And if you like your brown sauce you can do it, of course, again and again and eat like royalty used to all the time.)

Make a veal stock first. Ask your favourite butcher—you might need to go to a real one—for old bones and offcuts of veal. Rinse them, then cover them with cold water. Add a stick or two of celery, a few carrots cut up, branches of parsley, two well-washed leeks, a big onion (don't bother about peeling it, just quarter it), a big clove of garlic cut up roughly (don't peel it), a couple of bay leaves and a sprig of thyme, and bring it to a very gentle simmer, at which point it will sit happily for two to three hours. Strain it, and you've got your stock.

Now, the sauce. It's best made in a big heavy saucepan. Melt a big spoonful of lard—pork fat—in the bottom and fry in it a handful of smoked bacon (speck, kaiserfleisch) in short batons and another of peeled onion arcs. The bacon should be tending towards crispness, the onions translucent by the time you pull them out onto a side plate. This might take three minutes or so. Keep the heat going under your pan, because you're now going to add a heaped tablespoonful or two of plain flour to the bubbling lard and stir. The result might alarm you and look dark and disgusting. Stuff will stick to the bottom of your saucepan. Don't worry! There'll be fumes and you might even get some burning. Good. Keep stirring. Turn down the flames a little, but continue to stir until your fat–flour miasma turns the colour of an American basketballer. It will be arguing with you and it will also look unappetizing. But you're going to change that immediately by adding at least half a bottle of good red wine. A good strong shiraz is best, I think. Lighter reds will give you a less rich sauce. And please don't be tempted to add *el cheapo* plonk. It will just cheapen the king of sauces, which needs the best fabrics to turn out in his finest robes.

You let the alcohol boil out of the wine, even on high heat if you wish. This will take a minute or so. Then you throw back in your bacon bits and onions, fresh mushrooms cut up roughly, a couple of chopped and squashed garlic cloves, a chopped carrot, a teaspoonful of rich tomato paste and your veal stock, at least as much as the amount of wine you added. Fill your saucepan to the brim with it even, because you're going to let all this reduce over low heat and several hours.

And that's about it. Check your sauce constantly. Give it a stir to show that you love it. Get the gunk off the bottom of the saucepan into suspension in the sauce. Taste it continually, but you'll season it only when it's three-quarters done and you know you can't oversalt it. When it looks like lava, when it's chocolate-brown, when it tastes sublime, multifarious in its savours, as it will, when bits of vegetable matter are showing at the surface like stumps in a swamp, it's done. Strain it through a fine chinois, pressing the vegetables to release all their juices. And you've got a very great brown sauce. A *real* one. Taste it, and it will become your measuring stick of restaurants' efforts forever. Coat the bottom of a plate with it before you add a great steak, barbecued meats or anything in the way of fried or grilled protein. (It goes brilliantly with grilled tuna.)

Brown sauce—sometimes called Spanish sauce or sauce espagnole—is the basis for the greatest of haute cuisine sauces, those which require the addition of Madeira (you might like to try other fortified wines with it) or truffles or both to your basic brown. Demi-glace sauce is made by adding reduced veal stock to an already rich brown sauce. But the latter is already such a symphony of flavours that it can't be bettered, in my view.

A proper beurre blanc

'Beurre blanc' just means 'white butter', and this classic sauce has become one of the basics of modern restaurant cooking. Essentially, it means melting fresh cold butter into a flavour essence that you might have made from many ingredients. I'm not talking about the kinds of distilled tastes you can buy in small bottles such as vanilla or peppermint. I mean a usually cloudy, condensed liquid that you've made up to match whatever sort of protein you're going to pair it with on the plate. You'll see 'butter sauces'—the easiest way of describing them—with all sorts of white meats in restaurants, from chicken to seafood.

A classic beurre blanc, though, was designed to go with fish and is said to originate in Nantes in western France near the Atlantic. (You might occasionally hear it described as a 'beurre blanc nantais'.) It's a speciality, at any rate, of the lower Brittany region. Basically you boil together in a heavy saucepan equal quantities (you won't need more than a few glugs) of a very dry white wine—sauvignon blanc and marsanne work very well—and vinegar. (Again, it's your choice, but the spectrum you can choose from has bone-dry whites at one end and apple cider at the other.) From the start, chopped shallots, which give their wonderful characteristic flavour, and freshly ground black pepper are also in the mix. And you should boil these things quickly over high heat until you've got no more than a tablespoon of liquid when you strain it. (Press the shallot choppings to extract all the flavour.)

Many great sauces contain stock, and this one has fish stock—which you can simmer up from fish fins or carcasses or heads with carrots, leeks, celery, thyme, bay leaves, and parsley stalks. It should take an hour or more to make, just gently simmering away, taking flavour from the various elements and releasing it into the broth. Strain it, of course, when what you taste in the pot pleases you.

To your essence of white wine, vinegar and shallots you now add this stock—usually about twice as much in volume as the essence. The liquid will be translucent and have an off-white or creamy colour. Don't worry. Just taste it with a spoon and check out its wonderful spectrum of flavours. And when this is reduced—not by much; taste it—to your liking, add cold butter bit by bit. You might like to cut up your butter into small blocks before you start this stage of the process. And for these quantities you'll probably need at least half a block of butter in total. How much you add is up to you, of course; the rich fattiness of the butter should balance the sharpness of the essence.

Never let your butter boil! The sauce must remain opaque; it should never become transparent. Remember, this is a 'white butter' sauce, which means simply that the butter melts into the essence. Your burners should be very low as you melt the butter, and as soon as you've added a couple of dice melt more so that the temperature doesn't rise to levels at which the butter *will* become transparent. And as soon as you're happy with the rich flavour and smoothness of your sauce take it off the heat. The wonderful *Les Recettes Secrètes des Meilleurs Restaurants de France* ('Secret Recipes of the Best Restaurants of France') says this '*tour de main breton*' requires no great sleight of hand. You should however 'abandon all nervousness and work quickly' [my translation].

Beurre blanc was designed to be a fatty foil—as well as a flavour partner—to the stark, clean tastes of poached and grilled fish. Not fried or deep-fried things that swam, it should be added, where the double dose of fat would be cloying. So versatile and simple is beurre blanc that you see it everywhere. I've recently been served 'prawn' beurre blanc. Some are based on chicken stock. Melting butter into a flavour juice seems to constitute a beurre blanc, these days, so why not think up your own? Perhaps there's even a butter sauce that might be all-Australian. How about a 'beurre maroon' to go with kangaroo fillet quickly poached in strong stock? Its base could be a massive Barossa shiraz, 'roo stock and mango vinegar. Just add butter.

Joint of veal roasted over aromatic vegetables

It's a French classic to roast meat over aromatic vegetables. Ah, the aromatics ... Where would we be in cooking without carrots, onions and celery? They are the base of so much flavour-building, whether it's in stocks that become soups, sauces or stews or, as this article suggests, roasts.

Despite their universality, the aromatics do the best roasting job I've ever seen with a big joint of veal. Do enough homework, and you'll find a butcher who can provide you with a hindquarter or shoulder of true veal (*see* 'Veal blanquette'). Then, what you do with it will bring joy beyond belief. Perhaps into the afterlife.

I have never been to Albertville in the Savoie region of eastern France. So I've never eaten at the restaurant called Million, which had a Michelin star in the early 1970s when its veal roast won fame in the book *Les Recettes Secrètes*. Three decades later, I noticed, the Million had retained its star and, I'm guessing, but I'd bet my house on it, you could still eat a wonderful veal roast there. I've repeated the recipe many times at home without a single failure. It's simply wonderful.

Salt and pepper your leg of veal, rubbing the seasoning into the skin. In a moderate oven brown your roast in butter and oil, about three times the amount of butter to oil. The recipe doesn't say so, but this might take about twenty minutes. Then add to your pan peeled carrot batons, crushed and chopped garlic, half-a-dozen small peeled onions, fewer peeled shallots and—the single significant change from adding celery—three big tomatoes that you have peeled, pipped and quartered. And away you roast.

Les Recettes Secrètes keeps things simple, omitting that you might need to add more butter or oil. Also, the forty-five minutes in a moderate oven it specifies as a roasting time will vary significantly according to the size of your joint. I've had big legs of veal happily cooking for up to an hour-and-a-half in total. The book also neglects to say that you should baste your roast frequently, as you should any roast. But it does suggest that towards the end of the cooking you might like to cover the joint with aluminium foil to protect bits of it that are getting too brown.

Miraculously, the Million's sauce is simply the juices and sticky bits in the pan boiled with a little water until they form a light syrup. I also add some butter, which adds smoothness and body. Rest your roast, of course, allowing its juices to return to the centre of the meat, then slice it, serving it with the vegetables from the pan and your sauce. (Check the juice's seasoning.) Simplicity itself for a regal result, and for numerous wonderful tips on cooking and their principles, try to get hold of *Les Recettes Secrètes*, which came out in an English-language edition.

Red mullet

It's not until you have tasted them that you understand why little red mullet (species of the *Mullidae* family—the French name is *rouget*) are held in such high esteem around the Mediterranean. They are an exquisite little fish with their own special flavour. Twenty years ago in Australia they were a rarity, of goldfish status. In those days, real Aussies ate proper fish, which had to be big, preferably with endless rows of teeth and sandpaper for skin. And you had to buy them—or bits of them—deep-fried in batter. Red mullet might have sold well in bait shops. It's thanks to several well-educated European chefs—and a few Australian cooks who worked in Europe—that ordinary eaters have learned of the delight of this species.

There is a link between their size and sweetness, but don't get too carried away with it. The smaller they are, say some gourmets, the better they taste. But to get the best out of the fillets you're going to have to debone them with tweezers, so buying fish that are too small makes your work that much more finicky. Fish a hand-span, or even less, long are perfect.

Please leave the skin on; it has fabulous flavour. Once your fillets are deboned, feel for any bones you might have missed with your fingertips. The best and simplest way of preparing red mullet is probably frying in olive oil or other fats or combinations of them. (You might first like to dust them with plain flour.) Olive oil is simply traditional around the Mediterranean, and tradition usually means something is valued by locals not just over decades but centuries. And for very good reasons.

You won't get much more delicate flesh to fry than tiny red mullet. Don't overheat your oil. Your gas should be on low, the oil just searing to a bare knuckle. Put your fillets in the oil skin-side down. It's very important that you cook this side first, holding the fillets flat with a spatula if need be. If you don't do this they will curl, and proper cooking of the second side will be impossible. You be the judge, but it might be only a minute or so before you reckon they are ready. Then turn them over and cook the flesh-side for less than half the time the skin-side got. You might be happy with twenty seconds, say, depending on the fillets' size. Once they're done, get them out of the heat and onto kitchen paper to drain.

Your sauce could be anything you want to make it. A separate vinaigrette, a beurre blanc or even a dreaded emulsion from a jar. (But the last option is not recommended.) Red mullet fillets lend themselves well to fairly robust acid–oil emulsions because of their high flavour. Some French sauces incorporate the fish's liver, and others use fresh and dried herbs, which go marvellously with this species. (Mint, thyme, marjoram, rosemary and even fresh chopped fennel are all suggested.) In cooking red mullet, you should think robust flavours and a strong acid–oil combination.

In the late 1990s a friend and I took a daylong tourist cruise on a small yacht out of a small Turkish fishing port. Also on board were two crew and four tourists, who happened to be Turks visiting local relatives. From a distance, we noticed that the third-full nets the few fishing boats were pulling in contained fish that were more or less all the same size—miniature. Very few of them were anything other than silver. Even then, red mullet was becoming a rare enough delicacy in a particularly pristine part of the Mediterranean. 'And for lunch,' said the skipper, 'we have thirty or so little red mullet'—which he fried in a pan. The crew and the others showed little interest in them; I suspect only because they had them often enough. But my friend and I gorged till the last mullet was eaten.

Minutes-old salad from the garden

A friend of mine went into the Adelaide Hills to be self-sufficient. It changed his life, he said. Confronted with the need to kill living things to survive, he became a more humble human being. He grew his own vegetables and fruits, made his own bread, and killed and butchered his own animals of various sorts and sizes. It was all so very good for his soul, he reported.

The great French chef Joel Robuchon once sheeted home cooking and eating for me. Whenever we did it, he said, we killed other living things. The best cooks, he believed, were highly respectful of life in general. And no-one who has lived on an old Australian farm—or in an Italian village—can be unmarked by the distasteful, necessary and ultimately respectful ritual of killing a sheep or pig.

One of the notions that preoccupied me for many years was to be able to compose a whole dish of ingredients freshly cropped from my vegetable garden. (It would not require me to kill an animal, which I doubt I could do.) And I mean freshly cropped ... Minutes-old, preferably. I finally achieved it in the days when I grew my own wonderful grey shallots (their skins were brown), tomatoes (*see* 'A home-grown tomato'), and basil, both of which I still cultivate. There were usually enough plums (*see* 'My plum jam') to make my own plum vinegar, and I mixed it with virgin olive oil and splashed it over freshly sliced tomatoes, chopped shallots and shreds of basil. I speckled the lot with freshly ground black pepper, and I felt I was approaching urban peasanthood, that canny ability to live off the land.

I no longer grow shallots because they are cheap and ubiquitous in shops and markets, and several years have passed since I've made vinegar. I'm getting lazy. But lately there are good signs; I'm beginning to miss the pleasure of my tomato salad. I have two olive trees that might save me. I've had the first for many years, but it has suffered so many setbacks from having been moved that it is only now starting to look happy. In almost a decade it has produced about five olives. The second tree is only a hand-span high. But I'm hoping that at some stage in the future I'll be able to press my own olive oil. This will galvanize me to make vinegar, which should return me to growing shallots and combining them with tomatoes and basil. I'm hoping I'll get around to it before my demise.

Fried avocado

You're no doubt wondering if I'm mad. Yes, perhaps, but not when it comes to fried avocado. If any fruit is underexploited it's the avocado. They're plentiful and cheap, yet few chefs, let alone home cooks, seem to want to experiment with them. The enormously seductive texture of avocado has mesmerized them, I believe, and they can't see beyond it. Avocado has two uses in cooking, they think: you slice it into salads or alternate it with counters of crayfish tail. And that's about it. Well, I've got news for them ... and you, of course.

I began to experiment, believing that there had to be other things consenting adults could do with a ripe avocado. First, we should consider the

French way with them. Each eater gets half a fruit, seed removed. Into the hole left by removing the pip goes a fine vinaigrette (*see* 'A proper vinaigrette'). If you want to be posh about it you can add shelled crustacean tails, herbs, oysters or mussels out of their shells to your emulsion.

Then I asked myself if delicate avocado flesh would fall apart when cooked? This was a key question, I believed, because you encounter avocado rarely at a temperature higher than the ambient one. I put less than finger-thick slices of the great fruit on aluminium foil under a grill. What surprised me most was how well they retained their form and flavour. Curiously, they also gave off a whiff of fresh bacon—I'm not making this up—as they cooked. (A chemist could probably explain why.) And they tasted like ... hot avocado.

Slices fried in butter were far more interesting, reaching the gastro-hagiographic status required for inclusion in this book. I could see them served as a garnish just with fresh sea salt and a turn or two of fresh black pepper grounds. I could imagine them just as nicely—perhaps even better—dipped first in a light egg batter to create a kind of shallow-fried avocado 'chip'. And when I prepare an omelette these days, dice of avocado will often go in it with shavings of a great Italian hard cheese. Chopped leeks sweated in butter serve as an accompaniment.

Avocados are native to Mexico, and Waverley Root's wonderful read *Food* tells us that the name is a corruption of a short expression meaning 'testicle tree'. I've never looked closely, but apparently they grow in pairs. Root reports that the avocado was cultivated in Peru seven centuries before the Christian era. *Larousse Gastronomique* dismisses it in thirteen lines, sniffing that it is 'much prized by the Americans'.

In her *Encyclopedia of Food & Cookery*, Margaret Fulton more or less apologizes for them with a subheading 'Ways to Use Avocados'. Then she offers a lot more than most: half-a-dozen salads, a mousse, a soup (with chicken stock), a sauce, a dressing and baked avocados filled with 'creamed seafood, ham or chicken'. For all that, I'm still tempted to quote the song: 'Is that all there is?' And I shall most definitely keep on experimenting.

Steamed barramundi, preferably self-caught

Why self-caught? Because at least you'll be able to guarantee both its identity and freshness. Of all the table finfish in Australia, barramundi is arguably of the highest repute. And that means it's also the fish whose origins and authenticity are likely to be most muddied by the chain of commercial individuals between you and the estuarine water from which the specimen in front of you was alleged to have been taken.

There's another thing about barra. The quality of their flesh changes dramatically according to the season, and the best specimens are probably caught at the end of the wet, which is heading towards the southern Australian winter. After lots of feeding on insects and flushing with fresh water, they are supposed to come up a treat. I haven't knowingly known when most barra I've eaten were caught, so can't give you an opinion.

But I caught my own first barramundi at a time when the fish are said to be wilier, more slothful, and mud deposits in the gelatinous tissue at the base of their dorsal fins. It was for this reason, said my guide, quickly filleting the fish and throwing overboard the rest, that we didn't keep or cook whole fish during or at the end of the dry season.

The flavour and texture of ocean fish are, generally speaking, consistent and reliable. A snapper or red emperor or rock cod is never disappointing; their gastronomic attributes are consistent, provided the fish are fresh, because sea environments vary little throughout the year. Barramundi, on the other hand, live, depending on the season and rains, in the sea, in fresh water or a brackish estuary. Depending on climate, sediment and feed, their flesh can be pure white and gelatinous, or stringier and somewhat muddy. At the best of times, barramundi is a fish with lovely whiteness but a faint, rounded sweetness that takes some appreciation. To dine out on good wild barramundi your intelligence sources must be impeccable. Extract the truth from waiters with relentless questioning as to the condition and source of the fish. Many will give in and reveal that the 'wild' barramundi you will be served actually comes from a farm. The fish will have been artificially fed and grown to plate-size, not the metre-lengths the giants of the northern rivers attain.

At any rate, I brought back my first barra to Melbourne chilled. The first fillet, eaten that night, was excellent—if mild—in flavour. And I cooked it the simplest way possible, giving the fish's flavours the best chance to sing. In a big fish kettle I made a mattress of fresh 'soft' herbs from the garden—parsley, spring marjoram, a little mint, Vietnamese mint, and some onion shreds. I smeared a little good olive oil over the fillet, seasoned it and steamed it until slightly translucent juice began to emerge from the pricked flesh. Consumed the same way a week or so later, the second fillet, which had been frozen in the interim, was less good.

If you're interested in a more worked dish, you could steam your barramundi strewn with spring onions, discs of ginger, and sprinkled with peanut oil, Sino–Vietnamese style. Collect and reduce the steaming water while keeping the fish warm, add a little light soy sauce and serve.

Fresh home-made pasta

I simply will not forgive anyone who doesn't make her own fresh pasta—and blokes should do it, too—at home before dying. Fresh pasta is a universe away from its hard commercial cousins. In fact, it must be cooked differently and even *appreciated* differently. Let me explain.

Whereas commercial hard pasta eaten *al dente,* or firm on the bite, is largely fuel (carbohydrate) that is appreciated for the sauce that accompanies it, partly dried fresh pasta consumed immediately after brief cooking is pure sensuality. It slips and slides, twists and turns. It's unctuous on the tongue and soft between the teeth. Simply put, it's flour and eggs pole dancing. If you like sex, you'll *love* fresh pasta. It's terribly naughty stuff. Add sauce, and eat. (Have I convinced you?) To make it you'll need to buy a pasta machine, eggs and flour. The first mentioned might set you back up to a hundred dollars or so, but it will be around long after you're eating at the Long Table in the Princely Precinct.

I use a standard dough-making mix—nothing more than flour and eggs—recommended in *Pasta,* a twenty-year-old book I've got by that pope of Melbourne pappardelle, Tiberio Donnini. I also follow Tiberio's instructions. It's what you do with the flour and eggs, of course, that counts (as always), and occasionally—for no apparent reason—your best efforts get a poor result. (It's not Tiberio's fault, I quickly add.) So what follows can be seen, in part, as a risk-minimization procedure.

Break your eggs into a well in the flour in a large bowl. Whisk it all together with a fork, gradually ensuring this cloggy mess is fairly uniform, even if it looks nothing like pasta. Knead the dough vigorously using the heel of your hands for a few minutes. Try to form it into a ball. You're aiming eventually at trying to get a smooth surface and springy texture. Push a finger into it—it should emerge clean; the dough should be elastic, the hole quickly disappearing. If your dough doesn't behave all that well don't worry too much ... yet.

Turn it out onto a cold, flour-dusted surface (my stainless-steel benchtop is perfect) and knead it some more, turning it over on itself until it feels like a baby's bum and is of uniform consistency. By this stage, you will have noticed that even *making* pasta is a terribly sensual business. You find yourself tracing fingertips over the surface of your pasta perhaps more often than you should, and you hope no-one else is watching. You get out the digital camera and ... No, you don't, you don't do any of that. You just keep kneading. To reach the ultimate consistency and smoothness might take you twenty minutes, and when you achieve those aims your dough should be truly elastic. Let it rest under an upturned bowl for half an hour.

Tightly screw down your pasta machine, which will both roll the pasta into sheets and shred it into fettuccine or tagliatelle. Divide the dough into quarters and progressively roll each quarter into thinner and wider sheets. You'll know if your dough is any good at this stage: it can fracture along fault lines of flour; it can crumble; it can refuse to enter the rollers. Bad dough is smart; it spits dummies. Dough that is disciplined by enough kneading allows wanton and pleasurable manipulation. (You get out the digital camera ... I'm off again. Somebody help me!)

Let the sheets dry over the backs of bentwood chairs and broomsticks—whatever is handy—for a good couple of hours before shredding them. If you cook pasta that is too damp, the ribbons tend to stick together more than party members in an election run-up. Fresh pasta goes into copious salted boiling water, a little oil added, for three or four minutes. Test its texture as you go. Stop cooking when it's at its sexiest. (You'll know what you like. At this stage you might even want to ...) Drain well and add only the simplest accompaniments. A handful of freshly chopped herbs from the garden, olive oil and squashed, chopped and fried garlic go brilliantly. Add a grind or two of black pepper; get out the digital camera ...

Wok-tossed okra

Some funny people I know don't like okra. Yet I've watched as huge bagfuls of the stuff are tipped out onto the one and only okra bay at my local market—the hordes descend even before the Vietnamese bloke has finished emptying. Frantic hands dive in. It's a frenzy, I tell you, a bit like feeding-time at the zoo. And some of the hands scooping up the fresh pods belong to ordinary, everyday-looking Anglo–Celtic Aussies. (The better-dressed folk are always Asians and blacks.)

Okra is just fabulous stuff, and if you don't like its crisp, grassy exterior and slimy, gluey interior, which contains ball-bearing-sized white seeds, then read no more. Formally speaking, okra are the finger-length seedpods of *Abelmoschus esculentus*, a shrub that is one of a thousand species of the Mallow family of plants. (Among other members are cotton and hibiscus.) Indeed, a common name for okra is 'lady's fingers', and they are, indeed, best when they're harvested small and young. (Some imported okra preserved in cans and jars are only about a thumbnail in length.) The pods are pointed, most like a long, ribbed Noddy's cap. I've only seen them dark-green, but in some parts of the world white, red and purple okra are cultivated.

Sources say okra probably came from West Africa, taken to the Americas by slaves. Angolans are reported to have called it *ochingombo*, which became 'gumbo' in the States. And it's mostly known in the southern-US dish 'gumbo', an all-in stew that, in these days of spin, unsurprisingly often contains no okra. Sliced finely, it was originally employed as a thickener, its interior glueyness doing a wonderful job. These days, other thickening agents have taken over. Although uncommon as a separate dish, a Texan offering combines okra and tomatoes, and there is an okra pilau nicknamed Limping Susan. And in response to an article I once wrote about okra, readers inundated me with recipes, several of African origin.

The trick to making okra palatable for most people is to blanch it—after minimal topping and tailing—retaining crispness, but, more importantly, keeping its gluey slime inside the pod. Even large pods shouldn't be simmered for more than about four minutes. Once drained, you simply wok your okra quickly in peanut oil—other vegetable oils may also be used—with ginger, chilli, garlic, lemon grass, rice wine and soy sauce. Top with tear-ups of fresh coriander leaves.

Mâche

This stuff, you absolutely, positively must eat before you consume no more. I missed mâche so much when I returned to Australia from France that I began to smuggle seeds of it through Tullamarine customs on subsequent trips. Mâche is simply the greatest of green salad leaves.

In the past ten years or so insipid versions of it have become available in Australia, and several posh restaurants garnish mains with it or throw it in their salad mixes. But *la mâche* alone deserves your attention—just it, all by itself, in the ways I am about to reveal.

The short leaves of this salad do indeed have something of a lingual shape, and if you see it in a restaurant it will probably be called lambs'-tongues lettuce. (Just where you put the possessive apostrophe and whether you refer to one or several tongues is, of course, worth a best-selling book on punctuation. I understand, unfortunately, that someone has already written it.) It might also be referred to as simply lamb's lettuce or corn salad. There are several sorts of mâche, their leaves varying in length from about 4 centimetres (1½ inches) to double that. They will be from 2 to 4 centimetres (3/4 to 1½ inches) wide and come in a washed-out grassy colour or a very dark green.

The best size–colour combination is a small leaf of dark-green colour, and you almost never see mâche of this quality in Australia. So you might have to go all the way to France to enjoy it properly. I tried without any great success to grow it in my Melbourne backyard. French seeds were indifferent migrants, which didn't surprise me. They pined for the gentle undulations around Nantes (*see* 'A proper beurre blanc'), south-west of Paris, which is the origin of most of the 24 000 tonnes of the stuff grown each year in France. And mâche is a difficult salad; you must pull up the whole tiny plant, remove the root system and wash the rest very, very well. It has a habit of staying dirty.

But you *must* try it, as my introduction to this article insists. You will be gastronomically impoverished if you don't. This king of salads was first grown among vines or beside cereal crops before being taken up in peasants' gardens in the eighteenth century. By the nineteenth, it was well and truly established, and one source reveals that a famous unspecified Parisian restaurant created the 'Victor-Emmanuel salad', the protagonist of which was mâche (other ingredients were celeriac and beetroot), to honour Franco–Italian amity.

Eighty per cent of the Gauls say they eat it regularly, and consumption is increasing. It might explain why they are all so healthy. Mâche is rich in omega-3 fatty acid, folic acid, anti-oxidants, iron (equivalent to that in spinach), and vegetable protein, and it tastes grassy, sweet and nutty to boot. Toss it with your own vinaigrette (*see* 'A proper vinaigrette') made with a strong nut oil, such as walnut. It complements strong flavours. Alternatively, mince a hard-boiled egg very finely, sprinkling it over the top of your mâche leaves before tossing.

Fresh sardines

I'm not sure how good you are at martial arts, but threaten your local seafood purveyor with a big man's visit at the very least if his sardines are not fresh. Sardines—or pilchards, the preferred Australian marketing name—seem increasingly to be sold frozen. Or on the thaw. You know the sort of thing. When you bend them it's like listening to part of a glacier breaking off an ice shelf in Antarctica. Sardines are just not the same frozen and thawed. No seafood is, but sardines—pilchards—seem to suffer most deterioration. It's all right for fish shops to say the weather has been rough. My reply is that any excuse is a bad one, and frozen pilchards ought to be turned into fish protein for fattening other species. (Did you know some farmed chickens eat fish?)

Fresh sardines are wonderful, their flavour so strong, their flesh so naturally oily and resonating with goodness. Most people simply fry them, and there is nothing better. Gut them, behead them, flour them lightly, shaking off excess, and cook them in fat over moderate heat. They can be very brown and crisp on the outside without any damage whatsoever to the flavour of meat near the backbone. And, with this species, I'd recommend frying in butter alone. Butter gives them extra richness, and also tends to seal and brown the skin quicker. What goes with fried sardines? Great, fresh, chunky sourdough bread and terrific unsalted butter. (You'll want to season your sardines to blazes as you eat them.)

I hesitated only momentarily before adding another idea to this article: sardines escabèche. This latter style of treating fish has Provençal and Basque origins. You fry small fish, so why not sardines? I experimented, packing them after frying into a high-sided dish. Make a court-bouillon by boiling together vinegar, water (or replace this with fish stock), carrot discs, garlic cloves, onion arcs, celery bits, a couple of branchlets of thyme, two bay leaves, parsley stalks and seasoning. Pour over your sardines while it's still hot. Let the lot cool before putting away your escabèche in the fridge for at least twenty-four hours. Eat when ready.

Coral trout versus red emperor

By a short fat lip, coral trout just pips red emperor at the post. The contest? Which possesses the most exquisite fish flesh. And by the merest of margins, coral cod makes up a trifecta of warm-water fish of superlative flavour. Europeans and North Americans simply can't get hold of them. Provided we make special freight arrangements, we can buy these piscatorial princes even in the southern states of Australia.

Europe has its peculiarly petroleum-tasting sole, which it dotes on, its infamously tasteless sea bass and turgid turbot. As taste treats, our three stars of the tropics beat them to the bottom of the pool every time. First, they're big fish perfectly suited for steaming whole. Secondly, both the emperor and the trout are a fetching orange-red in colour, which can be maintained during the cooking. (Both the trout and the cod are attractively freckled.) Thirdly, their flesh is white and super-sweet—in the case of the cod it cooks into a lovely translucent soft gelatinousness typical of the cod cousins. But of them all, the trout just wins for its spectacular mouth-filling sweetness and wonderful white flesh flakes.

Procuring these fish straight from the water is going to be your challenge, because it's best to eat them as fresh as conceivable. (Catching your own is the best way to go.) And because of their wonderful characteristics and strong tastes, I wouldn't advocate any kind of culinary mucking around with them. If you're not going to steam them whole, then fillets can be lightly dusted with seasoned flour—more salt than pepper—before light frying in butter. Butter rather than other fats, in this case, because the richness of the dairy complements the wealth of these species' wonderful tastes.

Fresh wokked calamari

You'll notice already that I've suggested quick wokking and Asian vegetables several times in this book, especially to preserve the delicacy of seafood. And here I go again, advising you to pay the king of cephalopods this respect. How I'd love one of those turbo wok-burners you see in Chinese restaurants. You know the sort. The cook turns up the heat, the burner screams like a jet taking off and fierce spikes of flame sprout up well above the side of the iron. Such heat allows super-fast cooking, sealing in juices and flavour. It's said that for a wok to work it has got to be hot enough to make a bean shoot jive.

To die for

Your calamari should perhaps err towards a gavotte. Go the full squid with this one, too, buying your cephalopods fresh and whole. Don't buy rings, which are mostly frozen, and stew them for half an hour in a tomato-based sauce like the Europeans. We simply know better. And you will not need to tenderize them as some allegedly expert sources recommend. What heresy! And my last piece of preliminary advice is to be careful about what you are buying. There are squid and cuttlefish and octopus to contend with and they all tend to get lumped together. No-one on an Australian pier jigging a lure at the end of an amazingly long pole would agree with that.

Calamari is the king of cephalopod seafood, that's all—an exquisite eat you must try at least once in your life. Whole calamari sometimes frighten the average home cook, especially if he or she comes from an Anglo–Celtic background. Be not afraid! Their preparation is quick and easy. Essentially you pull the head, guts and tentacles out of the body pouch and use the tentacles and pouch for food. You might like to dissect out the ink sac from the head, but I don't because I don't like squid ink. Cutting the tentacles from the head is simple, but the body pouch, which contains most of the meat and makes the familiar rings, is a little bit more complicated. First, you feel for the 'whalebone', the corset that holds the calamari together. Ease the flesh from around it to expose a few millimetres, grasp, and pull it straight out. Then you peel the mucous membrane from the pouch to reveal the wonderful, familiar, off-white, translucent calamari flesh. Cleaned under running water, the squid bits are ready for slicing into rings or strips.

I begin by frying crushed and chopped garlic and fresh chilli in a vegetable oil before throwing in my rings, wetting the mix with mirin (sweetened rice wine for cooking) then soy sauce. You can add fresh ginger and lemon grass, too. Your rings will be done in a couple of minutes, depending on the heat of your burner—wait until their translucency is barely opaque. Then serve. Toss your hot calamari with fresh salad greens, if you like, and the result is equally sublime.

Officially, there are five sorts of calamari on the market—arrow, mitre, californian, southern and northern. Arrow (*Nototodarus gouldi*) is the catch in southern Australia and mitre (many species of the genus *Loligo*) swims to the north. The arrow has quite pronounced wings—the mantle—on each side of the body pouch, giving the back half of its body the shape of Concorde. Cooking it should be as sleek. And you can cook calamari on a barbecue, but remember those restaurant wok-burners and do it quick and hot.

Abalone various ways

For curiosity's sake more than anything, I'd like you to try abalone before leaving us. No way is better than any other, in my view, and while some fans of this gnarly, flat-domed univalve sing its gastronomic praises well beyond where you and I will both sit a century from now, I find them frankly disappointing. Their cloying taste has a touch of the vinyl in it, as far as I'm concerned. But try telling that to gourmets in Hong Kong or an abalone diver on Flinders Island. Indeed, in the former, abalone, sharks' fins, lobster and swiftlets' spittle are seen to be regal ingredients—without peer. And you could argue for hours about the relative merits of farmed or wild abalone, and whether they're better fresh, frozen or dried. On Flinders Island, the diver will be preparing his barbie, on which he will murder his catch, actually and figuratively.

Mind you, Australians used to call abalone mutton-fish, and probably treated them with the same offhandedness they reserved for the wether of the week chosen for slaughter. Their mild, nondescript flavour and tough, rubbery texture hardly compel you to make gastronomic allowances for them. Indeed, on Flinders Island a few years ago, I watched a man and his son take hundreds of dollars worth of this relative of sea snails from icy waters not much deeper than a man is tall. They were a short row in a dinghy from shore and stayed in the choppy brine for no more than twenty minutes. Then they treated their catch as if abalone were as common as eggs taken from under your backyard layers. Locals, they were allowed a limited catch of this alleged delicacy. (The waters of Tasmania, including those of the Bass Strait islands, are among the world's richest in abalone, contributing a quarter of the global wild catch. Fantasy sums are bandied about to buy a licence, which number something over a hundred.)

Most of the catch that day was black-lipped abalone (*Notohaliotis ruber*). Better-tasting, said the locals, were the green-lipped (*Schismotis laevigata*), which numbered only a few. The large grey central cylindrical muscle was shucked mercilessly from each shell, surrounding gut removed. Then each 'fish', as the Flinders islanders call abalone, was beaten viciously with an axehead, almost to a pulp. (I had no say in it—they had the heavy object.) Marinated in oil, vinegar and herbs for a couple of hours, the 'abs' were later 'barbecued' on a hotplate. Verdict? Nothing to write to the mainland about.

In Asian restaurants, abalone is treated with much more respect. (But I'm still dubious about the result.) I've tried it at one of Hong Kong's most esteemed Cantonese tables. Small 'fish' came in perfect form coated with a translucent gluey sauce. They had a stiffly gelatinous texture and a super-mild, smoky, plasticine flavour. Their taste needed acquisition.

Raw abalone? In a Melbourne sushi bar some years ago I noticed live abalones the size of large mussels suctioned to the glass of an aquarium. My young son tried a slice of one, sushi-style. I didn't like the way the flesh writhed as he brought it to his mouth. He found it amusing and ate heartily.

But it doesn't really matter what I think, does it? Abalone are huge. The Tasmanian industry, which is nearly double the size of Victoria's, was worth $128 million in 2000. Most of the catch is frozen or canned pretty much on the spot—after the divers are paid their 'beach' price of more than $50 a kilo. About three-quarters of it goes to Taiwan and Hong Kong. And poaching is a worldwide problem. Tat Sang Loo, a Melbourne kitchen hand, made more than $1.2 million in a year from abalone it was revealed when he pleaded guilty to fourteen charges in the Victorian County Court in 1999.

Abalone are not unknown in Europe. Channel Islands' 'ormers', as they're called, apparently an elision of the French *oreilles de mer* or 'sea ears', have been traditionally stewed. According to one fan, the flesh is exquisite and tender, the taste like veal. His recipe has you shucking the ormer, removing the gut, scrubbing the animal all over, pricking it on both sides with a fork and assaulting it 'heartily with a rolling pin'. (It staggers me that something as benign-looking as an abalone incites grown men to so much violence.) You then dry, flour, season and fry your ormers in butter until they're light-brown. Then you stew them for several hours in a seasoned roux (flour, butter and stock). You can't dive for Channel Islands' ormers, but if you follow out enormous spring tides you can simply pick them up. Restrictions apply.

In *Tastes of the Channel Isles*, Amanda Closs provides another version of stewed ormers called 'enne frichachie d'ormes'. Ms Closs adds bacon, mushrooms, herbs and gravy or stock to the ormers and bakes them covered for five hours or more. Yet another recipe has them stewed with carrots and bay leaf. Whichever way you choose, try them, but don't blame me if you're underwhelmed.

Fried eggplant

Eggplant—aubergine—is rarely subjected to culinary originality. We tend to see it cooked only one way, in a summer vegetable stew. And, of course, there is a host of summer vegetable stews. There's eggplant with tomatoes and onions. Tomatoes with eggplant, onions and thyme. Tomatoes with onions, eggplant, thyme and garlic. Even eggplant with onion, garlic, basil, thyme—and tomatoes, of course ... I'm sure you get my drift. Even in Thai food, dappled, pea-sized eggplant ends up contributing its flavour through braising.

Then one day I went to a Vietnamese restaurant and had molten, jade-coloured eggplant that had been zapped from above by radiated heat. It was brilliant, like seeing a dowdy spinster suddenly made over miraculously. The flesh of the fruit (that's what it is) was disgustingly sensuous. Good Catholics in the restaurant who had eaten it were contemplating confession.

And you can achieve this result at home quite easily. First, it's not possible to buy eggplants that are too big; this vegetable does not lose texture or flavour when it grows to XXXL size. Peel off the purple skin and cut up your eggplants into thick slices. Powder them all over with the cheapest salt in your pantry and let the slices stand in a bowl. After half an hour or so the bowl will be half-full with tea-coloured water that has been extracted from the slices. Miraculously, treating them in such a way doesn't make them oversalty; it just concentrates their mild and wonderful flavour.

Once the slices have disgorged their water they need to be dried with kitchen paper. A wily Croatian cook of my acquaintance taught me the next trick. Flour your slices, but not with plain flour. Use self-raising flour, she asserted, because it takes up less fat from the frying. (I'm no expert on the science of plain and self-raising flours, but I'll leave her idea with you.)

Using my granite mortar and pestle, I mashed up lemon grass, chilli, garlic and Thai basil from the garden and spread this paste very thinly over one side of each eggplant slice. I dusted them with the self-raising, shaking off excess, and fried them in a thin layer of simmering olive oil, turning them until they were brown. Crisp on the outside, of jade translucence within, they were magical.

Eggs benedict

For breakfasts and brunches, eggs benedict are beyond beating. Advertizing copy? Perhaps. But they're certainly popular for a reason. Every restaurant serving brunch seems to offer the benedict version of bacon and eggs. And to eat a really great version of this classic is to be transported stratospherically. There's the added rich butteriness of hollandaise sauce (*see* 'A proper hollandaise sauce'), and the foil of fine carbohydrate.

The quality of the muffins, which are specified for this dish, is usually where most versions of this dish die. Commercial bakeries bake terrible muffins. I can't say that too loudly. And if you can't get good muffins, you're not going to make good eggs benedict. Luckily, there are acceptable alternatives, bagels and brioche bread among them. So find the bread you'll like your eggs benedict to go on, even if it isn't strictly a muffin. And don't use muffins that are studded with dried fruit!

Then you'll need great eggs and bacon, which I know you can find. The hollandaise is going to be your challenge, but if you follow my easy instructions it should be excellent (*see* 'A proper hollandaise sauce'). The rest is really just constructing the concoction. Toasted and lightly buttered, half a muffin—or your choice of carbohydrate—goes on the plate first, followed by bacon fried in butter. I don't like it too crisp, but you might. Try to poach your eggs with as little vinegar as possible—or even none at all—in the water. If there's too much acid, its residual sting will be terribly pervasive. And always drain poached eggs well. At any rate, the egg goes on the bacon, and the hollandaise sauce goes on the egg.

I've read three origins of eggs benedict. In her *Encyclopedia of Food & Cookery*, Margaret Fulton says they were invented in a restaurant called Brennan's in New York. But dig a little electronically, and you'll be told they were conceived in the 1860s by chef Charles Ranhofer at Delmonico's in the same city. Mrs LeGrand Benedict, who ate at Delmonico's a lot, wanted something new for lunch. Or you might discover that it was created in 1894 at the Waldorf Hotel for Wall Street broker Lemuel Benedict. He wanted something to cure a hangover. I suspect eggs benedict will cure hangovers only if they are done brilliantly and you've drunk lots of water the night before. There is nothing curative in their physiological make-up.

And I should add my friend Robbo's version of the great benedict. Fairly logically, they're called eggs Robbo, and he poaches his eggs in strong chicken stock, which he discards after they're done. Moreover, his hollandaise is flavoured with red wine. It all sounds fine, but I take him to task about the chicken juice. It flies in the face of rule one of cooking: throw nothing out. So I've suggested he strain the stock after he has poached his eggs and make a butter sauce with it. Then you'd have a two-sauce eggs-Robbo-in-the-style-benedict.

— . —

Worth the effort

Judy of Sorrento's vanilla slice

Once upon a time, there were a million vanilla slices out there in the naked city. This is a story about one of them. Indeed, when I was young, the legendary Herbert Adams cake shops had two great winners. (Actually, there were several others, including jam rolls and sponges, but in small size there were only two.) These were vanilla slices and what were called neenish tarts, which, according to one source, were devised by one Ruby Neenish of Grong Grong, New South Wales, in 1913. Small round tarts, they contained a paste of icing sugar, butter and condensed milk, says Margaret Fulton, and were topped with a flat cap of icing, its two halves in different colours, either white and brown, white and pink, or pink and brown. They were disgustingly rich and sweet and, as kids, we loved them.

But back to vanilla slices. From reactions I've had whenever I've mentioned them in my writings, they are Australia's favourite cake. Yet they have a long history in other cultures, being essentially thin pastry sandwiching pastry cream. You can have endless variations on this basic idea, of course, and I recall that the pastry of Herbert's vanilla slice was fairly thin, compressed and flaky, and the filling a bright, buttercup yellow. Moreover, in texture the latter was unforgiving—stiffly jelly-like. And coating the top layer of pastry was white icing. Half-set.

In Victoria at least, bagging a great contemporary vanilla slice is a bit like duck shooting for gastronomes. Some slices have attained mythic proportions, such as the one that Mildura chef Stefano de Pieri drove hundreds of kilometres in north-western Victoria for to film for television. Ex-pat correspondents have written from overseas to tell me they pine for a particular version. One chap based in Indonesia said he used to buy a famous VS, to coin an acronym, on the western side of Lygon Street. (His remark, I felt, was a bit like saying you should bet on any Tour de France competitor who rides a bike.) A Pole once told me that locals descended on the Cracovia Hotel's pastry shop in Krakow to demolish 'napoleons', an heroic version of the humble VS with a dense filling of cream cheese between thin hard bicuits. It was similar to the Madonia Bros.' famous filled-on-the-spot cannoli in the Bronx, he added. Yeah, yeah, was all I could riposte. Another chap reported that his daughter had spent a year investigating vanilla slices in France. I wrote back to him saying that I hoped she'd filled in her time with other things as well. (The odd Gothic cathedral hangs around Gaul, and some nice pictures are on display.) But I got a real caning from a women from Ouyen in north-western Victoria (perhaps there's nothing to do up that way except bake) because I'd written about vanilla slices and not mentioned her town's annual Vanilla Slice Triumph bake-off. One of the judges, even, was former Victorian premier Jeff Kennett, a noted Melbourne gastronome. Hmmm.

There is a clear winner in the VS stakes, in my view. She's Judy of the seaside town of Sorrento, who daily in summer sells hundreds of slices from her gourmet shop in the main street. It's a huge block, her vanilla slice—two layers of fine flaky pastry (*see* 'Peter's flaky pastry'), the bottom one spread with plum jam, and the top one powdered generously with sugar. Between them is a rich snow-white cream. But wait around, because the filling is both a paradox and a stroke of genius. Instead of standard pastry cream, the guts of Judy Howarth's slice is a kind of dense white mousse that is light but deceptively mouth-filling. It's cool and smooth and barely sweet, which foils the sugar dust and the jam and suits our climate better than a traditional pastry cream. Sorrento is down south, and I've suggested to Judy that she enter her slice in the Ouyen culinary concourse. Can you imagine the civil war that would follow if she won?

Poached stuffed poussins

Poussins are baby chooks, and I know so little about sex that I've never been able to say if they're male or female. Spatchcock (which Methodists used to pronounce 'spatchco') was hugely popular with restaurants in the late 1980s and early 1990s and is supposed to be a baby rooster. But, again, my anatomical skills let me down. I was prepared to guess at the time that many 'spatchcocks' were of indeterminate sex. (Want a big job? Try chicken sexing.) There were possibly a few females thrown in as well, but it stood to reason that most of them should have been the real masculine thing.

Despite their fair degree of interchangeability, I've always thought poussins or spatchcocks were worth the trouble. Restaurants used to do them wonderfully, splaying them to plate size, and often marinating them in olive oil and herbs and a dash of something sweet. Then they'd be quickly grilled to produce lots of flavour and wonderful cooked-rare succulent flesh enhanced with the sugar of burnt caramel from the charred bits. Grilling properly indoors at my place is impossible; we have neither the stove nor the smoke-extraction capacity. So I usually poach or steam small-sized poultry. Poussins are ideal for the pot.

For a friend's fiftieth birthday I poached a poussin for each person. Being white meat, the babies needed something other than a brown sauce, I felt, which is made with red wine and forms the basis for the great sauces such as madeira or périgord. So, having started with the usuals (see 'A great brown sauce') of pork fat, bacon, onions and a little flour for thickening, I added about a third of a bottle of chardonnay. And instead of complementing this juice with veal stock I added about two cups of chicken stock. Other more or less traditional components included tomato paste, mushrooms, carrot, celery, garlic, parsley, thyme and bay leaves.

Once reduced over hours and strained, the resultant glossy, creamy liquid the colour of honeycomb had a well-balanced but enormously complex flavour.

Make sure you truss small birds well. What this does is retain succulence. If you let them cook untrussed, they'll set in ugly splayed postures, looking something like Jana Pittman hurdling. They'll also lose juice. And before trussing the poussins, I stuffed their body cavities with a blend of bread, onions, fresh sage and thyme, chopped crushed garlic, fried bacon batons, finely chopped celery, cream, cognac, seasoning and a whole egg. This was all done the day before, as a side effect of seasoning the inside of poultry is a slight desiccation of the flesh and subsequent flavour enhancement. Dryness is not your worry, especially if you're poaching, which I eventually did, quietly, for about an hour in a large pot of vegetable stock made from the usual aromatics and herbs. And I finished the sauce with butter and Madeira. The stuffing had a tasty moussiness, and the result turned out as well as I'd wanted it to.

Warm salad of bacon batons and 'wild' rocket

Menu-writers these days seem to have studied—all of them—a writing course of some sort, usually fiction. 'Wild' rocket is one of their favourite characters. Yet what is so wild about a green that has been cultivated for centuries? Like charity, rocket begins at home, where many people plant out a punnet of seedlings in spring. They reward the home horticulturist with a vengeance. First, you can tear the leaves off plants without seeming to affect their growth. Harvest what you need for the night's salad and your rocket plants do a Magic Pud. Fresh leaves ripe for picking will appear within twenty-four hours. (Until the plants begin to flower, that is.)

But the coin of rocket's power also has an obverse side. It runs rampant, self-sowing everywhere. And if you don't especially like rocket seedlings popping up in your lawn or between the bricks of your terrace or the tiles of your garden paths then don't plant it in the first place. I happen to think the gastronomic pay-off is worth it. It's great for its strong peppery flavour, the boost it gives to green salads even when it has to share the bowl with other leaves. And I love the way its flavour-character changes over the growing period. Early in the season, the spring-green leaves are succulent and less strong. At season's end, when flower stalks are shooting skywards, the leaves are darker, tougher and very strong.

Rocket does not captivate everyone. Indeed, many people don't like its unique spikiness, especially late in the season. Even if John Gerard in his *Herball* of 1636 thought rocket was a 'good salat-herbe', many later Englishmen found it inferior—'fetid and offensive' said one—and left it to the Italians. Being French, *Larousse Gastronomique* faintly praises it as a type of cress to use as an enhancer of salads.

It's from the *Cruciferae* family of plants, the leaves having alternating cumulus-shaped leaflets that merge at the top. Rocket is also versatile, being able to hold its own against other strong tastes, but also capable of foiling more subtle ingredients such as fish. I throw handfuls of it into chicken stock to produce a supercharged soup and add it to wok-tossings of seafood and other proteins.

Late-season rocket is especially appropriate in the following warm bacon salad, which is a kind of master recipe for all warm salads. (Just change the ingredients to create your own versions.) One of my many brothers-in-law— this one of Italian background—demonstrated it. Wash and dry your rocket leaves and put them in your salad bowl. Cut up cured pig of some sort—bacon, gammon, speck, kaiserfleisch, whatever takes your fancy—into short batons about 1 centimetre (1/2 inch) square and 3 centimetres (1 1/4 inches) long. Fry the batons in about three glugs of vegetable oil—use a couple of sorts, say a mixture of olive and peanut—until their outside surfaces begin to tan and bubble. Take the pan off the heat. Let me repeat that: TAKE THE PAN AWAY FROM ANY NAKED FLAMES! Because if you don't my next instruction is:

RING THE FIRE BRIGADE! Within an instant of removing the pan from the heat add an acid of some sort—it's your salad so you choose. (My own plum vinegar used to go very well in warm salads, but you might like to add apple-cider vinegar or even lemon or grapefruit juice.) Stir the pan vigorously with a wooden spoon, getting into suspension all the dried tiny morsels of caramelized meat stuck to its bottom. You should, too—and only experience will tell you this—add the right amount of acid to cut through the fat in the oils and bacon. Neither too much, nor too little. Actually, it's an outcome fairly easy to achieve and one with a wide margin for error. While it's all still warm, throw the pan's contents on to the rocket leaves and toss your salad.

Jacques Maximin's grandmother's rabbit terrine

Forget ferrets. When I was a kid on my uncle's farm near Melbourne—these days it's virtually a suburb—you'd send the dogs after rabbits. Norm always had a pack of bitsers, most of them small, but weren't they good at what they did! They'd chase the bunnies home. To their warrens. Using a shovel, we'd fill in all the holes but one, then dig the last hole out, removing cowering Bugsies at will. It was even easier than shooting them, which sometimes went on at night under spotlights, I'll admit.

Those great days of rabbit plagues and free protein have been systematically destroyed by pro-farming governments. (Or should I say pro-lazy-farming governments?) That Australia had a vast resource of real game that Europe would have gobbled up, so to speak, never occurred to them. Indeed, in the early 1990s I made a short spot for the *Sunday* television program about bunnies, shooters and a bloke on the Mornington Peninsula who each week was exporting to Europe and elsewhere containerloads of dressed 'burrowing lagomorphs' (I got that from *The Macquarie Dictionary*).

In Germany and France as well as other members of their esteemed European community, the demand still remains. But the supply, because wild rabbits are few and very far between, is extremely limited. And farmed rabbits—force-fed in cages—are bland, their muscle tissue not as taut or tasty as their free-ranging cousins.

Our wild rabbits, when you can get them, have become pretty expensive these days. But they're worth every cent of what you pay if you treat them right. In the old days, they might have been cheap and plentiful but no-one I knew cooked them well. They become inedibly dry and tough if they're roasted. And Australian stewed versions fail to enhance overall flavour, lacking a rigorous culinary approach. I remember that for the *Sunday* spot I helped a shooter's wife prepare her favourite rabbit recipe. It amounted to a gutted bunny rolled in foil with a quarter-carton of chateau cardboard red and a few shakings of dried herbs. A mate of mine of gastronomic pretensions once baked for us a brace of bunnies. His culinary technique rested on the dubious belief that the longer they stayed in the oven the more tender they became. Weren't true! They came out more tanned than a Mediterranean gigolo and tougher than his pimp.

By accident a few years ago I got a failsafe recipe for our wonderful wild rabbits from the esteemed French chef Jacques Maximin, who, last time I looked, headed up his eponymous two-star restaurant near Vence in the south of France. (Jacques was visiting Australia for some guest-chefing.) It was his grandmother's dish, he swore on his son's head, as Frenchmen do. Cook your rabbits in big chunks with bay leaves, whole black peppercorns and salt in a closed terrine filled with water in a bain-marie. That's all he said. It was a throwaway line as we parted.

I've tweaked his recipe here and there, browning the bits in butter first, which helps to keep the flesh together during two to three hours of cooking. I pack them fairly tightly in an earthenware terrine with peeled shallots, carrot slices, celery bits, a sprig of thyme and even a dash of white wine as well as

Jacques' grandmother's ingredients. (Bit of a lesson in apostrophes, that one.) Bake in a just-simmering water bath, ensuring that the bunny bits are submerged throughout cooking, which is completed when the meat can be easily detached from bone. Then refrigerate.

When you gorge on this delicacy you'll notice that marrow and joints have contributed natural gelatine, which results in much of your cooking juices turning to light jelly.

Steak and kidney steamed suet pudding

Let's hope you can fit a winter or two in before you pop off, because steak and kidney pie—or pudding, in this case—is the heartiest of eats. But you must cook it with suet pastry. 'Suet? Suet? What precisely is this suet stuff?' I hear you asking.

And well you might query it, because it's exceedingly difficult to find a butcher who can provide it these days. Suet is the waxy pure white fat surrounding animal kidneys, and in an era of meat prepared and packaged in warehouses for distribution to so-called local butchers, few retailers bother with this wonderful stuff. (And, of course, even fewer people are cooking with it, which is an enormous pity.)

Anyway, track down your suet—for enough pastry for a steamed pudding you'll need a good handful of it, which will be cheaper than a single boiled lolly. (A generous butcher might even give it to you.) A chunk of suet is made up of many small compressed fat lobes, and it's best if you remove as much as you can of the thin film (like plastic wrap) that surrounds them. Then chop your suet finely, flouring your knife so that it doesn't stick. Mix it with two cups of self-raising flour, salt and about half a cup of cold water and you'll get some pretty miraculous dough. Knead it well, rest it in the fridge for a while (say, half an hour) then roll it out. It will be amazingly elastic and unbreakable and studded prettily with pale-pink and white punctuations that remind you that a real live beast has contributed to it.

Steak and kidney filling can be anything you care to make it, based, of course, on fairly cheap cuts of steak and wonderful fresh offal. I've done one with a whole chopped ox kidney, stewing steak, leftover roast lamb (and the haricots that accompanied them), garlic, onion, carrots, lots of fresh parsley, rocket leaves, rosemary, half a bottle of pinot noir that had drunk well with the lamb, home-made tomato sauce, seasoning and a little plain flour for thickening. (If that doesn't stop a winter pang I'll cook for Bocuse.) I fried all these things using more suet, adding ingredients in the best order to maximize flavour. And there's a bonus when you cook kidneys: the glorious whiff of gramps's drying longjohns that invades the house.

I buttered and lined a basic aluminium steamed-pudding basin with the pastry. The basin had once belonged to my mother. Then I piled in the filling and sealed another thin pastry layer on top. I clamped on the lid and simmered the basin in boiling water for a couple of hours.

You'll turn out a perfect dome on to the centre of a large plate, a cupola that could compete with better-known ones such as St Peter's in Rome. (Or Melbourne library's reading room.) Lightly tanned, the pastry will be cakey and flaky and bready simultaneously, astoundingly digestible, and somewhat slimy where it meets the filling. And the latter will be simply wonderful.

Lamb's fry with a balsamic–basil reduction

Almost by accident, I found a use for that dreadful kitchen bully balsamic vinegar. It goes blindingly well with another great but misunderstood ingredient, lamb's liver. Or lamb's fry, as it was called when I was a kid. It was a cheap cut—throwaway, you might say, in a nation that fed off the roasted hindquarters of the best of the baa brigade at least once a week. For an unknown reason, my mother felt lamb's fry was a fillip before exertion and often fried it in dripping for Saturday lunch before I played football. The colour of a decommissioned battleship, its interior had a magical, yet unappetizing, chalky texture. Everyone appeared to be suspicious of everything in those immediate post-war decades and, in the case of lamb's liver, mothers probably feared liver fluke or something equally exotic that they'd heard rumours about. So they killed all possible pathogens by overcooking.

Yet when I began to eat underdone calves' liver many years later, I wondered if lamb's liver could be similarly prepared—take on a gastronomic quality it was never allowed when it was popular.

Even today it's shunned—and by chefs. I don't know why. I reckon it has huge potential to be an iconic Australian ingredient. With a tough sauce to foil its robust flavour, I believe it should have a gastronomic life outside the items in a country café's mixed grill that you leave for the kelpie by the fire.

So for the sake of experimentation I tried to buy lamb's fry. Fat chance! I had to consult three butchers before finding a lovely hepatic chunk. In cooking it, my attack, I posited, would be a kind of pincer movement from two culinary sides: I'd try to copy the calves'-liver-and-onion set piece; then I'd throw back to foie gras and partner lamb's liver with a vinegar sauce.

For trial one I borrowed from a northern Italian recipe. You gently sauté your sliced onions first in oil (I used butter as well to attain a higher temperature) for twenty minutes or so. Remove them from the pan, reheat the oil that remains and seal the liver. Return your onions to the fry-up and add some grated lemon rind. Turn down the heat, season, and simmer covered for three or four minutes. It's probably best to test the liver's doneness as you go. Mine was mostly just beyond pink apart from in the middle, and the result was OK if nothing more, the onions' sweetness outpacing the fry's strong minerality strangely enough.

Now for a gastronomic discovery of Einsteinian proportions. I sealed my second batch of liver in butter, removed the slices from the pan then deglazed the latter with a rich, fruity and quite old balsamic vinegar, letting it boil down to a fairly thick syrup. I returned the liver pieces to reheat them, added the juice of about a quarter of a lemon (to cut the big flavours all around) and freshly ground black pepper. And for good measure I threw in a handful of chopped fresh basil at the last minute. Eureka! Always a reserves' forward, I reckoned I could have made the seniors if I'd eaten this stuff. Proper lamb's fry at last!

Does the thought of eating liver repel you? My sources on cannibalism suggest that it's a huge delicacy among anthropophagists.

Brussels sprouts with nutmeg and cream

In the world's Anglophonic nations, the number of people who enjoy brussels sprouts can be counted on one hand. I'm among them. They are delicious, unique in flavour and texture, bitter yet fruity, and mouth-filling all at once. Indeed, I think their strength of flavour is what puts most people off.

By themselves, they *are* robust. I'm the first to admit it. But I'm convinced that Australians traditionally disliked brussels sprouts partly because of the way they were served at home. We had them boiled, and the smell pervaded the house, a portent to the awful moment when you actually had to sit down to a revolting mush, put it in your mouth, chew it, and swallow it, as my father used to exhort. On the plate, sprouts looked disgusting, too—a soggy grass-green miasma. You just knew they were going to be a bitter pill.

Then, many years later in France, I discovered that brussels sprouts could not only be edible but actually palatable, in fact one of the world's great gastronomic joys. French sprouts were no different from anyone else's. It's just that the good old Gauls never serve vegetables that are simply boiled. Apart from some special cases of partners to pot-au-feu and other 'wet' dishes, vegetables are always cooked twice—usually fried after boiling. And sprouts the French way were a delicacy.

You peeled off blemished outside leaves, made a cross in the stalk with a sharp knife and boiled them away to almost the routine mess Australians made. (About this part of the process I later became more critical, even if the sprouts retained a little of their crunch in France.) Then you'd drain them well, squeezing out unwanted water, which I perceived as a wholly innovatory move. Next came something even more foreign to a boy from Oz. Butter was set to bubble in a pan, small batons of bacon were added and fried to crispness, then the green vegetable miasma would be stirred into the lot. The result suited the strongest of meats, and clever chefs with French leanings have often in Australia prepared them thus to garnish game. (Even if they have only barely blanched them to begin with.)

Brussels sprouts are a very old vegetable; some sources date their cultivation in what is now Belgium to the late Middle Ages. They conquered the rest of Europe much later and, typically, Britain—which likes its food plain— was not a fan until the nineteenth century. (Yet sprouts are said to be exceedingly popular in England these days.) They grow well and are quite miraculous bearers. You break off mature sprouts only to have new ones replace them further down the thick stem on which they sprout.

And all this is well and good, but there had to be, in my view, a new way with sprouts. Margaret Fulton provided some answers, frying them (after boiling for about seven minutes) in butter, seasoning, lemon juice and parsley or cooking them in cream with white pepper. I liked the idea of adding dairy richness to them. It's a principle of cooking: you either foil a strong flavour with something lighter and sharper or go with the flow and boost heavy tastes with even heavier complementary ingredients. Experience shows you what goes with what. I tried cream and added grated nutmeg, another big taste, browning off the mix under grated cheese in the oven. It all worked brilliantly and was a meal in itself. A partner for guinea fowl, perhaps?

Roast leg of lamb with stewed beans

'What?' you gasp. 'Leg of lamb with beans? How could you? How dare you? Where are the roast spuds, the pumpkin and peas?' Er, well, they're absent, your Gastronomic Honour, because I was taught in France that only white beans (haricots) go with roasted leg of lamb. Only them. Nothing else!

Of course, this is nonsense, but it's Gallic nonsense, and when it comes to food the most outrageous nonsense propounded inside the French hexagon usually has some merit. In Australia, most of us think beans means a huge American transnational canner. But the more you cook beans yourself the more you'll find that canned versions are massively inferior. Home-cooked beans are an absolute treat for quite a simple reason. Pulses—seeds—are essentially bland. They amount to a blank canvas on which a significant palette of flavour-colours and complexities can be built. And in home cooking you never need to repeat a dish precisely—indeed, experimentation is half the fun.

It doesn't much matter what beans you begin with or, strangely enough, whether you pop them fresh from the pod or rehydrate a packet of dried pulses. You've got haricots, borlottis, limas and cannelloni, and the plainer and whiter they are the more chance you've got to show off what you're made of behind the burners. If they're dried, soak your beans overnight in plenty of cold water. I rinse them quickly after soaking, but some recipes insist that you cook them in the water in which they have been bathing.

Get a big pan and throw in any combination of fat you like—olive and other vegetable oils, butter, pork or lamb or beef fat from roasts (which I continually use in this way). Complexity is the goal, and the more ingredients we use the more kaleidoscopic will be our final flavour. (How do we know if it's all going to balance on the tongue? Taste as we go.) When the fat is very hot, throw in the beans, pressed and chopped garlic, chopped onions, carrot discs and smiles of celery. Fry the lot for several minutes. You don't have to turn anything brown. The idea is simply to make your ingredients sweat off some of their water, which has no flavour.

Now add stock—try always to have some on hand in the freezer. I've successfully used, for instance, juices from a corned beef boil-up or pot-roasted poussins. You use stock instead of water because it has intrinsic flavour, and flavour is what we're on about. Anyway, attempt to cover the beans and vegies with the stock and—but only if you need to—top it up with water. Add some tomato paste or fresh tomatoes if you like, bay leaves, parsley stalks and a sprig of a hard herb such as thyme or rosemary, and let it all bubble away until the beans are soft. Don't leave them underdone, a mindless mode in some top restaurants these days. And the good thing about beans like this is that you can reheat them until they're all gone.

And they *do* complement roast lamb, which I presume no-one needs coaching in. Or perhaps he or she does! One or two reminders about principles, at any rate, mightn't go astray.

I was quite horrified the first time I saw Frenchwomen stab their *gigots* (lamb legs) and insert slivers of garlic in the wounds. Why? Because when a joint bakes, tasty juice is driven out from its centre. If we're into flavour we should be into retaining it, and when your roast has anything up to a dozen gashes in it you're going to lose a lot of juice through the cuts. So, on this occasion, don't follow the French. If you want garlic or onion to add flavour, then put them in the roasting pan. There's no need even to peel them.

Smear your roast with salt and butter (you might like to stick with lamb fat, or dripping) and pre-heat the oven to a temperature approaching that of the core of the sun. After at most twenty minutes of this initial blast, your roast should be browning, its skin bubbling, and it will be sealed, the juices and flavours trapped for your pleasure. Then turn back your thermostat to a moderate heat and roast, never forgetting to spoon molten fat over the joint about every eight minutes. And turn it *without*—important this—piercing the flesh. (Use two big spoons.) A big leg of lamb will take a bit over an hour to roast, leaving its very centre warm-raw. Cook it more if you want it medium or well done. The French, by the way, roast lamb for far too short a time, leaving it mostly warm-raw throughout. I think it has far less flavour this way—and flavour is what we're on about.

Vichyssoise with seafood stock

Until quite recently, I'd never made a vichyssoise soup. The French classic of potatoes and leeks had mystified me. (But I'd also enjoyed it.) What was it about the blending of leeks and potatoes that created such a wonderful creamy, subtle alliance of mildness? I couldn't tell, but I felt that adding another understated taste to the mix could only enhance both the result and those who ate it.

Not so long ago, I found the juice from a mussel cook-up in my freezer. (Never throw away cooking juices.) I was aiming to make a classic vichyssoise soup and had no chicken stock. The bivalve broth seemed an interesting and appropriate—because of its mild flavour—alternative. According to Margaret Fulton, Louis Diat, a chef at the old New York Ritz-Carlton, created the classic vichyssoise. But its origins are in France's traditional leek and potato soup, called 'potage bonne femme' (good wife's soup). Indeed, I'd always thought it was peculiar that a French-sounding dish could be baldly named after Vichy, the Nazi's puppet capital. You won't find vichyssoise in Gallic cookbooks. Diat innocently named his creamy concoction after Vichy because he was born near the spa town. Some recipes for leek and potato soup add carrots and others add croutons. It's up to you what you do, of course; even whether you extend the soup with consommé, milk or cream. You might even like to add fresh herbs.

In essence, my vichyssoise went like this. I softened to translucency in hot butter without colouring them the choppings of two large leeks. Don't forget to wash them absolutely assiduously and use, depending on the colour and flavour you want your soup to have, the green tops. The more tops you use—I used about two-thirds of mine after trimming—the greener your soup and the stronger its leek flavour. I then added three medium-sized potatoes peeled and cut into big dice. Next added was my stock, which in volume amounted to about two cups. Already somewhat salty, this wonderful juice contributed all the seasoning the soup needed. It also added a palette of flavour-colours from the ingredients in which I had steamed the mussels—lemon grass, garlic, hard herbs such as rosemary, parsley, onion and even white wine (*see* 'Steamed mussels'). I boiled the lot until the potatoes were at smearpoint. Then a recipe will tell you to add milk, water or more stock. I chose about another two cups of full-cream milk, simmered the lot again, then blended it to a lovely pale and opaque peppermint cream. I served it that night, hot, with a dollop of fresh cream in the middle and a few choppings of parsley.

But the point of Diat's soup was its coldness. The idea came to him—again this is from Margaret Fulton's *Encyclopedia*—because his mother used to cool her soup with milk. Next day I pulled mine out of the fridge and tried it immediately. Amazingly, for something so cold, it had immense flavour.

Quails steamed in gin

In huntin', shootin' and fishin' days, quails might have gorged on berries in wild heath. They might have been, indeed, wonderful eating for their flavour alone. But perhaps no poultry have departed farther from their origins than the modern farmed quail. I'm not saying the latter are poor food—they obviously wouldn't be in this book if they were. It's just that you eat them mostly for the succulent jellied texture of their flesh, not any particular gaminess in their taste. Their flavour is attractive but very light.

In *The Birds of Australia* by Ken Simpson and Nicolas Day, I was surprised to discover that at least three species of these plump little ground-dwellers, including our own *Coturnix australis*, scurry through the heathlands of our wide-brown country. Being poor fliers, they lack the blood-delivery systems of other birds; hence their pale flesh.

Once, the *Coturnix coturnix*, or basic quail, was migratory in large numbers. In his 1973 book *Le Gibier* ('Game'), Paul Bocuse remarked that the birds island-hopped across the Mediterranean from Africa to Europe in spring. So tired did they sometimes become that they hitched rides on ships' bridges and even in the feathers of bigger migratory birds. (We'll believe it because Paul says so.) Winds were so strong over Bordeaux on 21 September 1888, cites *le grand* Paul, that there was a quailstorm, the little fellows literally raining down. Indeed, Waverley Root in *Food* quotes the great French gourmand Brillat-Savarin about the effects of prevailing winds on quails. Experienced gourmets could tell from the bird and the season whether it had been taken in a southerly or a northerly. If quails were flying into the wind they tended to rest more, fattening up on grapes and berries on the way. If they were flying with the wind they tended to keep going, toughening up in the process. So the story goes, at any rate.

Grapes are the traditional accompaniment for quails, but this dish has become so much of a culinary cliché that I don't cook it. The great film director Alfred Hitchcock is partly to blame. In *Frenzy*, the wife of a gruff London detective is driving him crazy. She's learning to cook at cordon bleu classes, and he sits down each night to small platefuls of badly prepared classics. After one especially hard day on the trail of a strangler he returns to find two midget quails and a few large grapes on his plate. The following morning the detective opines to a subordinate that all a British policeman needs is a hot English breakfast three times a day.

Escoffier lists seventeen quail recipes, but only quails with grapes seems to be repeated in *all* recipe books. (By the way, Escoffier recommends that roasted quails be first wrapped in a buttered vine leaf, a strip of pork fat covering the leaf.) Their delicacy does not warrant heavy sauces—or grapes, of course, which are too sweet. I pot-roast them. (And, yes, most Western brasseries marinate, splay and grill them. Restaurants of Eastern persuasions tend to serve them with a spicy salt.)

Truss the birds to make them compact, at least tying the legs together. Brown them in butter in a deep pan that can take a lid. Pour in a good slug of gin—an amount that would make a martini-drinker smile—and boil it off. Remove the quails; add oil to your butter–gin mix and fry small dice of carrots, celery and onion in the pan. This makes a rich vegetable mattress. Add some chicken stock to cover—just—the vegetables, then return your birds to the pan, resting them on the bed of aromatics with a herb bouquet and light seasoning. Turn down the heat, replace the lid and simmer. Test them after about a quarter of an hour. Turn them a couple of times to cook them evenly.

Pierre-Yves' brochettes of blackbirds and thrushes

Pierre-Yves would be late, said Colette, soon after we had arrived. He'd left that morning for the Atlantic coast to go hunting on our behalf. Oh, we said, in the stunned and apologetic manner of the new houseguests that we were. He shouldn't have gone to so much trouble, we added. Colette laughed, saying that her husband hoped to bring down a brace of wood pigeons for dinner.

Pierre-Yves was indeed late. But he made the two-hour drive back to the heart of Bordeaux by late evening. He had a surprise, he said. Blackbirds and thrushes! In three hours not a single wood pigeon had flown over. But there *were* plenty of blackbirds and thrushes, he added, and he'd managed to shoot enough for the four of us—exactly four birds each, surprisingly, two of each species. The Australians, even if one of them had been born in France, smiled, crinkle-mouthed. Sensing some apprehension perhaps, Pierre-Yves, who had been raised in these parts, assured us that we would *régale* ourselves, as the French verb goes. First, though, the small birds had to spend twenty-four hours ungutted and unplucked in the fridge.

Pierre-Yves gave up emergency medicine in Paris more than a decade ago for life in Entre-Deux-Mers, where he has a 300-year-old stone house and several long rows of grapes. For a while he was a worker-partner in a mobile wine-bottling business, but he recently picked up the doctor's black bag again. He makes about 1600 bottles of his own wine annually. But, above all, he is a dedicated hunter-gatherer.

From a high tower in the garden of a family cottage near the coast he brings down small birds with fine shot. The lead passes straight through them, he says. It's quite illegal, of course, even in politically incorrect France, and the towers are fast disappearing. But the local gendarme kindly arranges to patrol near his house only in the afternoons, when shooting is finished. (By the way, Bordeaux mornings in October sound like a war theatre. I've been in both, so I think I know.)

A couple of hours before cooking, Pierre-Yves gutted the *merles* and *grives* (blackbirds and thrushes to us, their unfortunate genus being *Turdus*), leaving in their livers. He'd learned these skills from his parents and grandparents, who were country folk. The tiny bodies were then skewered transversally, thick tickets of smoky fatty bacon between them. Then they were barbecued in the chimney over red-hot coals of Pierre-Yves' own dried vine prunings. Very big green Italian table grapes, pipped and peeled and fried in butter to a fruity, gorgeous and glutenous slag, accompanied.

Cooked through but sufficiently moist, the birds' flesh was deep mauve and chewier than quail, whose size they equalled. But, oh, the difference in flavour! These little blokes were liverish. (The livers themselves were too strongly flavoured for me.) You could taste the iron, which attested to their fast metabolism and energetic lifestyle. Most tender were the thighs, and cooking left fine bones edible. We ate by hand, obviously.

My standard reference on game cooking, Paul Bocuse's *Le Gibier* has fifteen recipes for thrushes and two for blackbirds. There's a gratin of thrushes, thrushes with foie gras, and stewed thrushes with juniper berries. Blackbirds are stuffed with grapes or juniper berries. None of the recipes is as simple as my friend's, which, the more I thought about it, was an unusual and very un-Gallic way of doing things.

Fresh green peas

Who got the peas that rolled onto the floor in your house? The dog? Or were they squashed under foot? Almost no-one shells fresh peas any more, and you really should have a last fling at it. It might even become a habit.

There is really nothing like fresh green peas. They are amazingly sweet—seem sweeter than the sugared variety from a can—and have a terrific chlorophyll taste. Indeed, no other food I know, certainly not dried pulses, seems to signal as much concentrated potential for life—sheer vivacity—as peas from the pod.

It's alleged that we all hate the labour required to shell them. But decades ago, when we were children and it was said to be a chore, shelling peas was actually fun. It's for obvious reasons that people say an act is as easy as shelling peas. They ripple out like creek water over stones. I wasn't alone in spilling them for fun, I'd guess. Didn't they bounce on the lino! We'd have to round up every last one, sometimes even those that the dog had sampled and spat out. You'd also find amazing grubs in some of the pods ... and smear them.

These days, fresh peas seem smaller and less uniform in shape and size. I got only about two-thirds by weight of peas from a recent market purchase. The biggest were about the size of what we used to call peewee marbles. Without handpicking fat pods with thin shells this is what you're reduced to. I also don't agree with the French that smaller peas are sweeter, *pace* the Gallic obsession with petits pois. God knows peas are small enough when they're large. And the theory that the less smooth they are the better they taste sounds as if it comes from a book of Eastern European culinary myths and legends.

I ended up with half a colander of peas, at any rate, and adapted the advice of Escoffier, the man who established modern French culinary tradition. He lists five ways of preparing them. Lettuce figures in three of them. Only in 'English' peas (with mint) and 'Flemish' (with carrots) is it omitted. Just why it was decided that lettuce went with peas I am yet to discover.

But I went for broke, adding not only a whole butter lettuce but two small carrots (in batons) a large onion (in arcs), a crushed garlic clove, two teaspoons of sugar and a large parsley stalk going to seed. They simmered for about twenty minutes, and the result was delicious. In the last few minutes of cooking I drained off most of the juice, which I used later to cook pasta. Big knobs of fine butter were stirred in, and black pepper was freshly ground over the top just before serving.

One of the most ancient of vegetables, peas are supposed to belong to only one species, *Pisum sativum,* which has many varieties. They are thought to have originated somewhere between the Middle East and Asia. And your classic folk, those Greeks and Romans, used them dried, not fresh. Thankfully, we're somewhat more enlightened.

Veal blanquette

I had the great pleasure many years ago of taking to lunch the formidable French pianist Vlado Perlemuter, who had met Ravel and become perhaps the greatest exponent of his keyboard music. In Melbourne for concerts to celebrate a particular Gallic festival the name and details of which entirely escape me, he was so traditional a man, I'd been told, so set in his ways, that he would probably appreciate only his homeland's cooking. So I booked a well-known French bistro with a reputation for doing, all things considered, an above-average job.

A charming, stick-thin septuagenarian with a lightly ironic expression playing about his lips, he insisted on beginning with the 'freshly' opened oysters. I told him it was a mistake—we just don't treat oysters well in Australia (*see* 'Freshly opened Pacific oyster')—and detailed what he was likely to be served. He'd give them a go nonetheless, he smiled. Sure enough, he brought the first New South Wales rockie to his old lips and sucked, expecting to taste the wonderful liquor the bivalve lives in. To his surprise, he vacuumed plain air, the mollusc dead in its half-shell. Well-mannered despite this letdown, he hoped the veal blanquette would be better.

'Blanquette de veau' is a Gallic classic, cooked by all Frenchwomen. (French men, in general, don't cook all that much.) And if you look up their traditional recipe books you'll be instructed that real veal comes from an animal slaughtered at between two and three months of age. The meat should be white-pink, have little odour and a fine grain. And, of course, veal has a characteristically mild but persistent flavour quite unlike that of beef.

The blanquette arrived, looking very much like the real thing, apart from one essential ingredient, which I hoped the maestro might fail to notice. Perlemuter forked in, chewed and swallowed. Not bad, he said with a little smile. Not bad at all. I smiled back. There was just one thing, he added, leaning forward to whisper. They hadn't broken an egg into the blanquette at the last minute—like his mother used to do.

Like several concoctions, veal blanquette unites the erotic and the gastronomic. In taste—and even textural—terms, the raw egg stirred into the stew just before it's served adds very little. But the egg's protein coagulates with the heat of the stew to form semen-like streaks through the meat, carrot and onions. I've mentioned this to no-one—you're the first to know—but a lot of France's libertine ways can probably be sheeted home to eating occasional veal blanquettes in the privacy of the family home.

It's an easy dish to do and you really should surprise yourself with it. You begin with very good veal—it doesn't really matter which cuts—that can be sliced into large boneless chunks. You soak these pieces of meat in cold water for at least half an hour. This softens textures; whitens the meat; hydrates the veal somewhat, which sounds quite ungastronomic but hang around for the denouement; and rinses away any extraneous blood.

Drain the meat, and cover it with fresh water in a heavy saucepan with a few glugs of white wine, rounds of carrot, arcs of onion, seasoning and a bouquet of fresh thyme, parsley and bay leaves. Bring the water to the boil, skim the foam carefully off the top, and simmer for ninety minutes to two hours. When the meat is soft—the initial soaking probably lengthens this process, helping to tenderize the meat—strain off the cooking juices.

Combine equal smallish quantities of butter and flour in a heavy saucepan over heat and add your cooking juices a little at a time. Cook the resultant translucent, claggy sauce for at least ten minutes or so; you're aiming for thickness and to ensure that the flour is digestible.

Put your sauce back in with the meat, carrots and onions and stir to form a rich, stiff stew of exquisite flavour. Don't ever forget, though, that, at the moment of serving, you have a duty to *la France sensuelle*, a *duty*, I say, to drizzle raw egg across the top and stir. Hide the slime with chopped parsley if you're at all prudish.

To die for

Coq au vin

Ah, Mrs Beeton, Mrs Beeton ... Where are you when we need you? Myth has it that, in her book of 1861, the great Isabella directed the assiduous home cook first to catch her chook. The myth is wrong. Actually it was a hare for jugging that she instructed her readers to snare, a significantly more challenging task than pursuing poultry in a pen.

Or so I thought. But I was reminded of Mrs Beeton as one of my several brothers-in-law in the early 1980s first tried to catch his rooster. Or, our rooster, because we were going to make coq au sang (rooster with blood sauce), another of the great Gallic gastronomic gambols and a brother to coq au vin. We were making little headway. I don't think Pierre liked this particular cock, and I'm convinced the rooster didn't like him. I vaguely recollect that it had savaged him or his wife, my wife's sister. At any rate, the rooster swaggered around his chookpen in a chipped-stone village outside Paris as if he owned the half-dozen or so layers that shared it with him. He probably did. And, on this particular occasion, he was in no mood to get caught. He squawked and flapped, ducked and weaved, and dealt glancing blows to our calves and ankles as he feinted.

Man won in the end, of course, and Pierre eventually cornered him and caught him. It looked like a fight in a pub. The rooster was tied upside-down under the eaves of the carport. The rest of this article will now be rated X. Read no further if strong violence offends you.

Pierre went into the house and came out with, still in its packet, a chrome-plated secateurs-like instrument with a wide scything blade and a cup-shaped cap opposing it. He needed it specifically to cook coq au sang, he said, retrieving a battered aluminium basin from his garden shed. The idea was to get the blade inside the rooster's beak then squeeze. The cap came down and pressed the rooster's palate against the blade, which penetrated the brain, causing instant death, according to the instructions. But the implement was strategically designed also to allow a free flow of the *coq*'s best blood, which would spatter into the basin, then eventually thicken the sauce.

I watched Pierre do it, my only thought being that his courage was greater than mine. The rooster flapped up a typhoon but Pierre hung on, perhaps half a small cupful of the bird's precious bodily fluid dripping into the basin positioned underneath. None of us should ever forget that preparing animals to eat is a brutal and often disgusting business.

We all scalded and plucked the rooster, and what surprised me most was the amount of vermin he hosted on or near his skin. Then he was gutted and cut up for the pot. And was quite tough and unappetizing, as it turned out, even after he was cooked.

Now, I don't want to suggest that anyone put him- or herself through the ritual of cooking coq au sang. But a proper coq au vin is a joy. It should begin with a big old roué of a chookpen rooster, which is almost impossible to obtain in Australia. A substitute big boiler will just about do. And the important thing to remember about rooster in wine, to translate the dish, is that you make it the day before you eat it. For a very important reason.

First, you brown off your pieces of poultry with chopped onions in butter. Powder some plain flour over the top and cook all this for a few minutes. The bird bits will appear as if they're covered with a kind of translucent lumpy slime. Heat up some cognac in a small pot, set it alight and pour over the top, before adding at least half a bottle of a good pinot noir, seasoning, and squashed and chopped garlic. Simmer all this for at least an hour. (If you don't have enough liquid to cover the chook add more wine or a good poultry stock.) Turn off the heat and leave your *coq* alone until the following day.

Half an hour before serving, reheat the dish, adding small batons of smoked bacon, small onions fried in butter and mushrooms of some sort. Check your seasoning and serve. Right through to the bones, your poultry pieces should be stained a pale maroon colour in homage to the wine; they should also have a deft, complex but heroic flavour. Most coqs au vin served in Australia are usually devoid of these characteristics. I've no idea why, but I suspect it's laziness or a wish not to cook something the day before if it is going to be tabled commercially. Indeed, in my earliest reviews I took restaurants to task because the red wine had failed to colour the meat properly. Follow the procedure above and it will.

A boiled egg

What are boiled eggs doing among allegedly more difficult culinary dishes? The French have a saying they use on people—usually family members—who are pestering them: 'Go cook an egg!' What it means is that you've got too much time on your hands, you're annoying me, and boiling eggs might look simple but if you do it well it's going to get rid of you for at least a certain time. And if you can boil an egg well, the result is heavenly.

Three minutes simmering? Well, yes, but ... It depends on many things, doesn't it? The freshness of your eggs, their size, the amount of water in your pot, and, if you want to get technical, the altitude at which you are boiling them because this affects temperature. A very outdated but reliable cookbook I turn to for reminders about traditional techniques offers three ways of boiling an egg: lower your eggs gently into boiling water and simmer them for two to three minutes, withdrawing them immediately after; lower them gently into salted boiling water, cover the pot and take them off the heat, allowing them four to five minutes to cook; or put them in cold water over medium heat, and when the water boils they should be ready.

So good luck at going and cooking an egg. I'd only add that it helps if your eggs are at room temperature to start with: cracking and those puffy, awful clouds of white are less likely. And you should add just salt—and perhaps freshly ground black pepper—to a boiled egg. Butter if you want to be lavish. And please use the best and freshest eggs you can afford.

A grizzling *pied noir* woman's real couscous

The qualification—and implied recommendation—in the above heading I make with some trepidation. They're specified in spite of a dramatic and amazingly painful incident I once endured. Many years ago my wife and I had a friend who was born and raised in Algeria. European Algerian, she—and her parents and grandparents before her—were proud *pieds noirs,* the slang expression for Europeans of North African birthright. Her elderly mother, who visited Australia every so often from France, where *pieds noirs* habitually sought refuge following Algerian independence, was an expert at making couscous. And we were inveigled into eating the real thing one momentous night.

And along with the meal you got, of course, a stream of racist grizzles about Arabs in particular and sundry other North Africans in general who had taken her country from her. It was a kind of constant background music to what began as an absolutely delicious treat.

Essentially a spicy stew of lamb and chicken accompanied by steamed beads of millet or semolina (what we call 'couscous' but what is really only the carbohydrate component of the dish), a real couscous has many elements. First, there is the cooking juice of the stew itself, which is served separately as a soup. Then there are the pieces of mutton and chicken that have simmered for hours with aromatics, which include carrots, onions, chilli powder, tomatoes, celery, bay leaves, herbs such as parsley and thyme, and a sachet of spices, including black peppercorns, cloves, cinnamon and cumin. Quartered artichokes and chickpeas, turnips, beans, marrow and zucchini are also in the mix. Usually, the meat and vegetables are served in separate bowls. Garnishes always include chilli powder or paste or, indeed, fresh chillies.

Then there are the small globules of steamed grain themselves. *Larousse Gastronomique* goes into considerable detail about the possible origins of the word 'couscous'. It might be a Gallic corruption of *rac keskes*, which in one North African dialect means 'crushed small'. Or it might be a phonetic version of any number of possible transcriptions of the name for an earthenware pot. This latter has holes that allow grain to be steamed when it's set on top of another containing boiling water or stock. Still other sources believe 'couscous' is simply onomatopoeic, resembling the sound of steam passing through the holes of the cooker. If you look around North Africa or French flea markets you might come across a real *couscousière* (couscous steamer) in elaborately etched brass. Properly steamed grain should never touch boiling water. These days we empty a packet of couscous into just-boiled stock and stir.

And the grizzling *pied noir* woman's couscous was brilliant, the stewed meats and vegetables so tasty and exotic, the steamed grain wonderfully light and fluffy. To a background diatribe about the deficiencies of *les Arabes*, I was urged to have a second helping. Then a third. Washed down with a sturdy shiraz from northern Victoria, I ate on, oblivious of the danger. We got up from the table properly satiated—we had been fed like Bedouin royalty—and went home.

Now, steamed grain sometimes has a tendency to continue to cook, I believe. And a couple of hours after I had finished eating, I became a human *couscousière*. The semolina expanded inside me. I expanded with it. The pain was excruciating. And this torturous chastisement for blatant greed continued for something like six hours. Naturally, I failed to sleep. I nearly failed to live.

I've been careful ever after when eating couscous. But, gee, it's wonderful stuff—all of it, in all its various parts and versions—in the mouth. So much so that from 1975, when immigrant workers' families poured into France from Tunisia, Morocco and Algeria, North African restaurants specialized in couscous. Look around Paris next time you're there. You'll see the word 'couscous' more often than 'coq au vin'. Despite their xenophobia, the French themselves—from students to *PDGs* (managing directors)—have come to love the stuff. It has arrived on the menus of company canteens and schools. And a survey in June 2004 ranked couscous the Gauls' fourth-favourite dish. (Mussels, veal blanquette and pot-au-feu—boiled beef—pipped it.) The French eat 75 000 tonnes of couscous a year. Australians are some way behind still, but then we never lost a colony, never had to backtrack from any haughty pronouncements about Algeria being French, never had the right background music to go with it.

Bisected baked scampi

Just for a challenge, I've included scampi among your comfort-food dishes. I believe it's the greatest of crustaceans—its flesh sweeter and much more delicate in taste and texture than any variety of prawns or crayfish (southern rock lobster) you care to name. I'll be taking scampi sandwiches on my long journey to the afterlife. So delicate are they that the animals are frozen immediately, I understand; they deteriorate rapidly if they travel fresh. (Perhaps a test beyond even the scope of this book might be to join a deep-sea trawler some time between now and your demise and cook just-caught scampi on its pitching deck. Now might not *that* be a sublime gastronomic experience!)

We call them scampi, but in Europe they're known as Dublin Bay prawns, deep-sea prawns, Norwegian prawns or by their French name *langoustines*. And they're easy to identify—good specimens grow to about 20 centimetres (8 inches) in length, and they have a uniform delightful pale pinkness and long thin claws. Most scampi eaten in Australia come from deep waters around New

Zealand, but trawlers haul in significant numbers of *Metanephrops australiensis* from muddy bottoms of the Indian Ocean and Timor Sea off the north-west coast of Western Australia.

Scampi are so revered by chefs and gastronomes that you will see myriad recipes for them in restaurants around the world. Cooks in Italian *tavole calde* (cafés) tend to smother them in a sauce that usually contains tomatoes. And French recipes tend to overcook them with the usual culinary culprits—garlic, shallots, cream and seasoning. But their flesh is too delicate, too sublime to be worked hard. It's a sin, I tell you. We have more respect for food, I trust, than to allow that.

So I'm urging you to adapt a recipe that initially astounded me when I ate it years ago at the first Tetsuya's in Rozelle, long before Tetsuya Wakuda became world-famous. He warns, by the way, that the secret to successful scampi is rigorous undercooking. He splits his scampi down the middle, and seasons them with salt, white pepper and finely ground Celyon tea—just a sprinkle. Then he pops them into an extremely hot oven, taking them out after about three minutes or just when they feel hot to touch. Their flesh should still look a little translucent. He dresses the crustaceans with a flavoured 'scampi oil' made from the shells fried with aromatics such as carrot, celery and onion. And his garnishes are again more complex than you will need to use to astonish your friends and neighbours. You could even get away with a spoonful of great vinaigrette (*see* 'A proper vinaigrette').

Gratin dauphinois

Countless are the ways to cook potato, but preparing a real gratin dauphinois should be one of your main culinary aims before you can no longer grasp a peeler. It's so unctuous and filling in the mouth that even the most minute oral cavity seems to be flush with this wonderful creamy stuff. And it's extremely easy to do well. Strangely enough, it's also easy to turn out quite ordinary examples of a dauphinois.

The key thing, as always, is quality ingredients. Get good potatoes. There is always an argument if I suggest one variety over another, and I've never logged the potatoes I used when I had my greatest dauphinois successes. So experiment. Where I live, we tend to use firm waxy spuds of medium or higher price. Don't get the cheapest, and don't use any that are soft or growing shoots. You might like to ask your greengrocer for his suggestions. When you slice them into discs, at any rate, your peeled spuds should be so crisp they sputter juice.

The procedure from then on is simple. You take a deep-sided oven dish and smear its bottom and sides with crushed garlic and butter. Then you build up, layer by layer, the slices of potato and more crushed and chopped garlic, grinding black pepper onto the layers, and adding rock salt (be careful not to oversalt) and even knobs of butter if you like richness. Boil a saucepan of full-cream milk, and, off the heat, melt some grated cheese into it. Some traditional recipes might also advise you to stir in a beaten egg (wait for your milk to cool considerably), which will give your dauphinois a more jelly-like—rather than creamy—texture. I decline the egg, because I prefer the cream. In my time, I've also enriched the boiling milk with pure cream. At any rate, when you have a rich dense fluid, pour it over the potatoes. Cover the top with a thick layer of grated cheese—you can use just about any hard cheese but the textbooks recommend the great gruyère—and more knobs of butter.

Into a hot oven goes your dish, cooking for around three-quarters of an hour. The dauphinois' surface must be fairly resistant and mid-brown. It's hard to overcook and dry out a dauphinois, so you may continue to cook it—causing the potatoes themselves to take on a thicker, creamier texture—covered. Give the dish five minutes uncovered at the end, though, to brittle up the surface.

To die for

Dominique's crème caramel

One of my wife's best friends was among the most beautiful women in the world. She came from Madagascar, where her father was a vanilla exporter. We were never privy to the rich cocktail of blood that made her, but it produced a rare example of the tall, the dark and the exquisite.

And she would ply us with fresh vanilla beans—or freshly exported, I should say, because vanilla beans come from afar and are processed. And my wife Dominique would flavour her crème caramel with them.

I shall never forget the perfume of Yvette's pods. Unrolled from their waxed-paper wrapper, their redolence filled the kitchen. Moreover, they seemed to contribute flavour and fragrance inexhaustibly; we used the best of the bunch every so often over several years, keeping them between-times in the fridge. A hand-span long, wrinkled, dark-brown, their surface the texture of a dried date, the pods were lightly frosted, a sure sign of their superlative quality.

In *Food*, Waverley Root devotes more than four pages to vanilla. It's one of his longest entries. He reports that it was discovered by the Spanish in Central America. Apparently, the Aztecs mixed it with chocolate as an after-dinner drink. The Spaniards, no doubt dazzled by all these new flavourings, were more inclined to dose their bedtime cocoa with cinnamon.

Root reports that the three species of the *Vanilla* genus are actually climbing orchids with tendrils as long as an Olympic track sprint. At first resembling green beans, the seedpods turn golden yellow, chocolate brown then almost black. They're picked just before they're ripe. This uses enormous amounts of labour, of course, which is necessarily reflected in vanilla's price and the large market in ersatz vanilla essence.

Freshly picked vanilla pods are fairly odourless, but fermentation brings out the best in them. *Larousse Gastronomique* says that they're plunged briefly into boiling water and sealed in tins before they're dry. Over time they develop microscopic vanillin crystals, which look like a kind of fine powdery coating. Split the pods when you use them to release minute specks, the vanilla's seeds. They'll fleck your custard or crème caramel, stamping it with authenticity.

Vanilla-speckling made its biggest impact on me in 1987 at Jamin, Joel Robuchon's wonderful Michelin-three-starred restaurant in Paris (*see* 'Joel Robuchon's mashed potato'). I couldn't believe his crème brûlée's sensuous power. Then, near the bottom of the bowl, I saw speckles the size of dust caught in sunbeams. When I remarked about them, Robuchon said simply, '*Drôle d'effet, eh?*' (funny effect).

Dominique's crème caramel is a world-beater, not only because of Yvette's wonderful vanilla beans. She concocts it with a kind of zealous precision, as if she were making it for a restaurant. That's why it's so good. First, she confects her caramel from about 200 grams (7 ounces) of sugar, a little water and even less red wine vinegar. These things are heated in a heavy saucepan until the caramel turns dark tan. But don't cook it too much, even if you are effectively near enough to burning it making caramel. When it's an almost unpourable tanned syrup, tip it into an oven dish—in which you're going to bake your crème caramel—and roll it around so that it covers the base completely and comes up the sides about two-thirds of the way.

Now, bring to the boil about four cups of milk containing your vanilla pods—put in a couple for strength. While it's heating, blend half a dozen eggs and about 200 grams (7 ounces) of caster sugar in a bowl. When the milk is about to boil over, pour it into the egg–sugar mix and whisk it vigorously. This will become your gently gelatinous crème when it's cooked, so some people pass it through a strainer before pouring it into the oven dish. Dominique never has, and produces every time a crème with a mirror finish. At any rate, the crème goes in a bain-marie into a medium oven for about thirty to forty minutes. Take your crème out when the top is brown and it wobbles when you shake it. It will

To die for

set beautifully when it's cold. Put it in the fridge, take it out some hours later, and turn it out of the dish by running a knife around the edge. Put a plate over the bowl, quickly invert the plate and dish, and the crème should drop out. It's good if it is uniformly smooth throughout—not even the tiniest bubble.

One day, going on holiday, Yvette and her two children were killed in a road accident. It was in all the papers. Her husband was driving behind, saw the carnage, and cradled his dying daughter.

Obviously, we no longer get Yvette's vanilla pods, but each of Dominique's crèmes caramel, I like to think, is something of a memorial to the wonders of women in general, and, in particular, to a very special, very beautiful daughter of a vanilla trader.

Brent's pavlova

As the great Ernest Hemingway would have said, it is good for a fine man to make a good pavlova. But, then, I suspect Ernest never ate one in his entire life, let alone cooked the great Australian dessert. (Too busy leaping on the pigeons in the Luxembourg Gardens.)

Now in youthful middle age, my friend Brent, who is still alive and channels his creativity into cooking and not writing, is a very fine man who has every right to be mad, bearing in mind the magnitude of others' problems he listens to each day in his line of work. He is also a pavlova champion. He hasn't had a failure, he tells me, since he began baking them at the age of ten. His French–Canadian mother gave him the recipe he uses, although what she was doing with it he declines to reveal. He alleges she cut it out of a women's magazine. (Quebec's esteemed monthly *Cuisine Australienne Aujourd'hui?*)

Brent's pavlova begins conventionally. He beats the whites of four big eggs into a very stiff-peaked foam. A cup of caster sugar is folded gently into it. I suspect he does this with the same care he employs to probe the intricacies of disturbed minds. He adds a tiny glug of white vinegar and several drops of vanilla essence. He spoons his mixture on to a foil-covered tray, mounting it as high as he can. If your pav's plateau can be at least half a hand-span high you are likely to succeed, he says.

The pav goes into a hot oven to bake for fifteen minutes. Then turn the oven off, but leave the pav in. And 'Don't stickybeak!' as Brent exhorts, for at least two hours. Take it out, turn it upside-down onto the serving dish, and peel off the foil.

New Zealanders get hurt when Australians clutch pavs to their bosoms. It's true that Kiwi-folk had always baked small meringue cakes before World War II when the pav was conceived. But they did not create the great Aussie culinary icon. That was left to a shearer's cook of Germanic background to think up. I'm indebted to Michael Symons' *One Continuous Picnic* for the following story.

Bert Sachse, previously of the Barossa Valley, walked off his wheat farm in Western Australia in 1926, an early victim of the Depression. His wife Mary was quite a cook, and she and Bert opened a restaurant and pie shop at Mullewa, several hundred kilometres from Perth. Mary was terminally ill, they had four daughters and a son to support, and she felt Bert should know how to cook as well. So she taught him. When a passing team of shearers needed somebody to stoke their boilers, Bert took the gig. He eventually left the men in singlets behind to become, initially, a passable hotel chef. But by 1934 he had exceeded his own expectations by ruling the burners at the smart Hotel Esplanade in the Western Australian capital, which was as old as he was—thirty-six.

The Esplanade's afternoon teas were very fashionable, and its licensee, Mrs Elizabeth Paxton, decided one day to value-add—and super-please her patrons—by offering something new and very special in the pastry line. With her manager Harry Nairn, she approached Bert, who thought he might try to improve on earlier efforts at meringue cakes. It had irritated him for years that they were hard and crusty. He was reported as saying that he set out 'to create something that could have a crunchy top and would cut like a marshmallow'.

He experimented for a month, eventually achieving the classic pav by adding cornflour and vinegar to whipped egg whites. When presented with the new confection, either Elizabeth or Harry remarked that it was 'as light as Pavlova'. (The great ballerina had danced once in Perth in 1929, two years before her death.) Whipped cream and passionfruit were Bert's accompaniments from the very start.

And in that most Australian of cookbooks, *Encyclopedia of Food & Cookery*, that canny Scot Margaret Fulton leaves out the cornflour. Like all things to do with pastry, sweetness and eggs, it's a difficult bake. Fulton gives separate protocols for gas and electric ovens. Cooking with gas, she says, you use the lowest temperature and bake your pav for ninety minutes. In an electric oven it takes half that time, but you must turn the oven off and leave the pav in with the door closed for a further hour.

Have I confused you sufficiently? I'd only advise you to give Brent's pav a go, as much as I like Margaret. He advises that the topping is up to you. 'Anything creamy you like' suggests a man built like a green bean. He endows his pavs with sliced banana, sweetened whipped cream, strawberry slices and 'passionfruit drizzled all over'. (It's all right for some. If you want to eat Brent's pav and stay thin, join him on his marathons.)

I feel it's time we took pavlova beyond traditional realms of cream and passionfruit and explored newer culinary fields. (I haven't run the following suggestions past Brent, mainly because he has always found me a suitable case for treatment even without my corrupting the great dessert.) Why not try clotted or pure creams? Or mascarpone? Or cream cheese and a sweet fruit such as guava? Or why not spray liqueurs straight onto the pav then follow up with real honey or treacle and cream? Or why not cover the top with thin slices of caramelized apple and blast them with radiated heat or a blowlamp? And has anyone made a non-sweetened pav? On which I'd put, if I made one—which I haven't—a layer of parmesan and blast it quickly till it melts. I'm sure pavlovas can be pushed exponentially, culinarily speaking.

And for those of you—like me—whose pavs constantly fail, Brent has a final piece of advice. You must beat the eggs to very stiff peaks, and your oven must be very hot when the pav goes in.

Mrs Weiniger's chicken soup

Perhaps this little gem shouldn't be in the 'harder' home-cooking category at all. After all, chicken soup is chicken soup, except when the Marx brothers make it with duck. No, Mrs Weiniger's chicken soup is hardly revolutionary at all. Chicken, schmicken!

And if you adopt that approach, there's your first problem. You don't shop after a *particular* chicken like Mrs Weiniger does. In her eighty-seven years she has never found it harder to get a good bird. But she looks and looks with the help of her only son, my friend Peter, who went on to become something even more important than a doctor. (A journalist.)

She didn't ever need to cook as a girl in Vienna. But when Hilde and her new husband, Kurt, escaped to the French Concession in Shanghai (later to be rounded up by the Japanese and restricted to a guarded compound for three years where their son was born), she learned to prepare chicken soup. The family lived in a single room and Hilde cooked over a charcoal burner. Her chicken soup was concocted not from a recipe, but from the past.

So we sat one recent *Shabbat* morning and began with Mrs Weiniger's liptauer—a kind of cream cheese and butter with paprika and chopped capers—on toast. Then we ate chopped liver—a pâté of chicken livers, onion and chicken fat—on toast. Then we revelled in Mrs Weiniger's chicken soup, and she told me what went into it.

She bought only free-range chickens these days. Poultry had seen better times, she reminded me. The leaner the better. And she adds to a good chicken in a pot the usual aromatics—celery, carrots, leeks, garlic and lots of parsley. And that's about it, apart from *at least three hours* simmering. Chicken soup is always made the day before, she adds, and when you take it out of the fridge you skim any fat off the top before reheating and serving.

With matzo balls, of course. And she makes them with a cup and a half of matzo meal, which looks like coarse breadcrumbs, three eggs, olive oil, salt, chopped parsley and half a cup of warm water. And the result is truly wonderful, the soup pale khaki, translucent, parsley-flecked, delicious on the palate, and singing not so much of any particular flavour as a kind of atavistic perseverance. I had a cold and within half a day this 'Jewish penicillin', as it is known, had cured me. (Mind you, I think the experience had something to do with it as well.)

'What happens to the chicken?' I asked. Mrs Weiniger was faintly dismissive of my question, but admitted that she makes a sort of risotto for the grandchildren, who love it.

She can't understand people who use stock cubes to make soup, and she will keep on making it her way, thank you, even if the years are catching up with her. The other day, for instance, she woke up worried because she couldn't find her pills. After an hour of searching for them she relaxed. She realized she wasn't taking any. That she thought she was on medication when she wasn't, though, unsettled her a little. Thus is older age.

Now find your own Jewish grandmother.

Peter's flaky pastry

A lot of cooking is alchemy. Some people can do it and some can't. Two people can stand side by side. They can use identical ingredients. They can follow the same procedure. One will conjure something sublime. Another will produce ... Pastry forgives you least. I can't cook it. I've tried and tried, and watched my brother-in-law Peter do his flaky version in wonderment. I've listened intently to his teacherly tutoring, his attempts to show me how. Then I've failed.

It irritates me like you wouldn't believe that he can do it consistently well, too. He never fails. I wrote a kids' book (never published) that said cooking was an enchanted kind of art. One of what E. M. Forster would have called the 'round' characters in the narrative, a grandmother and a fabulous cook, says at one stage that she can't understand why she cooks so well; the magic just comes out through her fingertips. Peter is like that. When it comes to pastry (and a lot of other dishes, I should add) he's got it. I haven't.

For a while in the late 1970s I used to call him BYPIA, the Best Young Palate in Australia. He runs the boarding house of a famous school and teaches English and literature. But his flaky pastry exceeds anything else he does. Any restaurant in the world would be delighted to table it. It's unnatural. The gods infiltrate it. Peter insists that this is rubbish, of course, but I'm not so sure.

Flaky pastry—*pâte feuilletée*—is at the pinnacle of French cuisine, the most elaborate of the pâtissier's skills. Essentially what you do is make and roll out dough, fold it around butter, rest it, roll it out again, rotate it, fold it and continue this process in such a way that precisely 729 micrometrically thin layers are produced when you bake it. The great French chef Antonin Carême said it was important that 'this paste ... neither be too firm nor too soft—it should be just in between'. He went on, 'It is, however, better for it to be a little on the soft side rather than too hard.' I hope you understand.

Peter says it took him years to get it right. You start off with equal weights of flour and butter. Mix a quarter of your butter with all your flour and half the weight of flour in cold water to make the dough. Peter adds a few drops of lemon juice. The hard stuff comes next. After resting your dough for half an hour in the fridge, you roll it into a perfect rectangle like an A4 sheet. You blob the top two-thirds of it with a third of what's left of your butter, fold the bottom third up over this and the top third over the back of the bottom third, just as you would a letter.

After more fridge rest, you turn the block of paste through ninety degrees, roll it out into a rectangle, refold it, turn it ninety degrees, roll it out and incorporate the next third of the remaining butter in the same way you used the first third and rest it again. After yet more fridge rest, you do this one more time to exhaust your butter. (And possibly yourself.) There are some crucial rules. Rotate the paste in the same direction. Dough and butter must be of equal temperature and similar consistency. And each time you roll out your dough you must make a perfect sharp-cornered rectangle.

Peter uses his flaky pastry with steamed asparagus spears, for instance, but I especially like his apple tart. He rolls a sheet of flaky pastry into an A4-sized rectangle. Retaining a decent border around its edges, he fills in the 'canvas' with peeled and sliced apples that he sweated the day before in butter, cinnamon, gratings of nutmeg and cloves. He rolls out a second sheet the same size and a bit thinner. He wets the border of the first sheet and gently presses the second sheet over it—over the apples, too, of course. He trellises the top decoratively, brushes on a beaten-egg glaze, and bakes his tart for forty minutes in an extremely hot oven. It's wonderful.

Anyway, *bonne chance* with *pâte feuilletée*. With a bit of luck, you just might have the touch.

Karen's Christmas pudding

Physical density is an interesting concept. It's all about how much mass is in a particular volume. Some experts say—at least I think they say—that some pinhead-sized points of the universe contain the combined mass of whole galaxies. I never believe too much to do with outer space, believing that the sky is probably painted on a huge backdrop a couple of hundred kilometres above the Earth. Who did it and why I've never bothered thinking about. And what is beyond it I don't care.

I believe things in front of me, and Karen's Christmas pud is believable only because—like Everest—it's there. It is quite simply the densest entity in my known universe, containing within its normal puddingly dimensions a whole galaxy of gastronomy. And all she says is that she follows a recipe that appeared in a metropolitan newspaper many decades ago. I thought no-one enjoyed the years in which I grew up, but those who cooked Karen's pudding must have had fun. At least on 25 December.

A couple of years ago, Karen and I had a Chrissy-pud contest. She won. And I'd gone to so much trouble with mine. Here's what I did.

First, I read several recipes for Christmas puds. It seemed to me that a handful of ingredients—suet, treacle and bicarbonate of soda—were unlikely to be included in most modern versions of the classic. Knowing I wouldn't have to reproduce the pud precisely ever again (and knowing that something similar would be equally good if I did) I borrowed from several lists of ingredients. I ended up with sultanas, raisins, mixed dried fruit, powdered spices, bicarbonate of soda (an oldie but a goodie), eggs, plain flour, northern Victorian port and muscat, rum, breadcrumbs made from stale bread, suet (the pure white fat surrounding kidneys, see 'Steak and kidney steamed suet pudding') and treacle. I measured nothing except the quantity of flour, judging by guesswork what I thought was the right amount and tasting afterwards.

There are many ways of putting these things together, but I just blended them in a big basin and sat them in the fridge for twenty-four hours. Puddings of this sort should be boiled in a pudding basin or scalded muslin for anywhere between three and eight hours. I had a feeling mine was done in five-and-a-half. Made several weeks before Christmas, it was reheated in its muslin cloth for a further ninety minutes before being served. Excellent, it was still not up to Karen's. Here's what she does.

Being the kind of honest gentlewoman that she is, she first acknowledges the decades-old recipe that appeared under the hand of a great cookery writer, Geraldine Dillon. Ms Dillon was the kind of cook who urged you to check the raisins for any seeds or stalks and to break up clusters of sultanas and currants. These vine fruit, at any rate, are mixed in her recipe with chopped blanched almonds, an apple, half an orange, mixed spice and nutmeg to create the basic flavour. Of course, the usual suspects that give body and rise and lightness—self-raising flour, breadcrumbs, sugar, eggs and butter—are added in abundance as well. But I had better straightaway say why Karen's creation is better than even Ms Dillon's probably was in its pure form: she leaves out the mixed peel. She just doesn't like it, she says, and in omitting it perhaps fruit density is increased. (If you think I'm no astrophysicist, I'm also no horticultural expert.) Never use packaged breadcrumbs, exhorts Ms Dillon, and I suspect Karen agrees, producing them with a blender and stale bread. The Dillon–Karen pud is cooked for four to six hours, depending on the size of the basins in which you're producing it. Moreover, the pudding is boiled for a further two to three hours before serving. I don't need to repeat how magisterial it is.

And, finally, why don't plum puddings contain plums? Scour the literature and you'll find Margaret Fulton referring to 'plum or Christmas puddings' but listing the usual plumless ingredients. My ancient *Green and Gold Cookery Book* cites two readers' recipes for 'plum pudding' and 'Christmas plum pudding', both devoid of the fruit. Surprisingly, only that terribly Anglophobic publication *Larousse Gastronomique* includes plums—in the form of prunes—in its Christmas pudding recipe. (It also devotes almost half a page of fine print to a rather tortuous routine for preparing pud before a throwaway note at the end says that 'the making of plum pudding is simple and easy'.)

Fresh pork sausages

Now, I'm cheating here a little. While I long to make my own chunky pork sausages at home, I haven't yet acquired the equipment. I will, don't worry about that. It's just that with this one you could very easily beat me to it.

I like fresh, proper sausages so much that I learned how to make them in a restaurant kitchen—La Luna's (see 'La Luna's pasta marinara'). Chef-owner Adrian Richardson has been producing magnificent house-made snags for many years—they sell like house-made snags, a minor truckload of them exiting La Luna each week either in stomachs or as takeaways. He took me through the whole process.

We made two sorts—a beef-and-pork and a pork-only. For the beef sausage he used trimmed offcuts from the aged steaks he butchers from carcasses stored in his coolroom. The pork is super-fresh and has a clean, floral yet characteristic smell. He uses meat from what he calls the 'barrel' (chest and belly) of the animal. It might also come from the neck or even the leg. There is a cardinal rule, though: the protein must be of high quality. The better the meat the better your sausage. Long gone are the days when butchers made their sausages out of what was swept up off their floors at closing time, sawdust and all. Anyway, the beef is trimmed of any nerves or gristle; the skin and stringy bits of pork are removed. And you're left with a pile of meat cubes, each about the size of two matchboxes. And perhaps the most important ingredient to have a sufficient quantity of is fat: about ten per cent of the beef-sausage mix is fatty pork, and about a fifth of the pork mix overall is fat. He judges these things by eye these days.

The moisture content of a fresh sausage is vital, says Adrian. To the beef mix he adds roasted field mushrooms that have thrown a lot of juice. He feels the wetness before the meat is minced to check that it's right. You're unlikely to get sausage-making right first time, he counsels. But by about your third or fourth go you should be producing a highly edible confection.

Adding the correct amount of salt to your meat is essential. It heightens flavours, but also has the key job of preserving the meat. Adrian reckons it's easy if you've got a calculator; you add 1.2 per cent by weight of salt to your mix. He's not really fussy about the type of salt you use, and you can obviously experiment. And that's the very basics of the mixture. He goes on to add heaps of very roughly chopped fresh parsley, thyme and whole big leaves of fresh sage. As well as the herbs, fennel seeds go into the pure-pork snags. And freshly ground black pepper and a few garlic cloves are added.

Another important thing to do is to work quickly. When he makes his snag mix, all the meat comes straight from the coolroom at a temperature most of us couldn't match at home. Protein begins to coagulate with heat, as we know, so if you work cold your meat is going to be in the best possible shape when it gets minced, which heats it slightly. There's a mantra sausage-makers chant: the three 'Ks' of sausage-making are Kwick, Klean and Kold.

You can use a hand grinder or buy a smart electric one, which might set you back up to a hundred dollars or more. But Adrian recommends that we all fall back in love with our local butcher and I heartily agree. Most alleged butcher's shops these days are retail outlets for meat that has been prepared elsewhere. Don't go to them; use a real butcher. Search long and hard enough and you'll find one. If you take your meat-buying business to him, he'll be happy to run your sausage mix through his mincer—keep it chunky, please—and also turn it into sausages using real intestinal casings. Try at home by all means, remembering that practice makes perfect, but you might have to practise harder in your own kitchen to make well-formed sausages.

When they're done, dry them on a wire rack in the fridge for a day before using them straight away or storing them in batches in the freezer. To thaw, simply bring them to the boil then cool immediately under cold water or ice.

You can barbie snags, of course, but if you've gone for fat ones—which I think is the legitimate way to have a sausage hit—you might want to fry them in butter in a pan that can take a lid. Once browned, add a little stock or wine—the normal stuff or even rice wine—and cook with the lid on for ten minutes or so over the lowest heat. Ah! Heaven in a pork balloon.

— . —

Perfect 10s

Murray River pink salt

There are salts and better salts, and about the best I've tasted—and that includes the grey *fleur de sel* from Brittany—is the palest of pinks. It's called Murray River Gourmet Salt, and I neither have shares in the company nor am I paid to promote its products.

These tiny, flaky curls are more or less addictive. It's an effort of will to stop eating them. Whereas most salt has a very sharp palate finish—as it should—that wrings the salivary glands of their juices and makes you want to rinse out your mouth, the Mildura product has a curious fullness and seems made for eating.

Launched early this century, the Murray River company used to produce salt only for industry; owners of livestock and swimming pools were its main consumers. But then managing director Duncan Thomson thought of trying to make a truly gourmet product from an easily accessible resource, underground aquifers only a few kilometres outside the north-western Victorian city. Pumps lift heavily saline water and run it into natural basins for evaporation. The resultant salt is harvested and taken to the company's factory in Mildura itself. Here, it's blended with other mineralized brines that are extracted from the aquifers, evaporated again and dried to produce the salt's characteristic taste and tint.

The recipe and the process, which took two years to refine, are both secrets, says Duncan Thomson. But he'll reveal that calcium, potassium, magnesium and iron are some of the elements that go into the blend. In short, it's a natural mineral cocktail. He could produce versions of any of the great gourmet salts, he says, but why should he when he can do something unique? And even better.

A home-grown tomato

Does anyone need convincing about this one? I think probably not. Ask the avid home gardener why she keeps a vegie plot and she'll invariably say she can't buy real tomatoes any more. How true!

You don't need me to tell you how appalling retail tomatoes are. They have been bred for the convenience of capitalism, if I may get a bit bolshie. Tough skins and solid flesh have been selected genetically. Taste, which in tomatoes means ripeness and therefore softness, has been progressively eliminated. (You might also have noticed lately that some tomatoes are kind of squarish, so that they can be more easily packed and stacked.) In the late 1980s I was given, for tasting, a new tomato bred by a laboratory to retain robustness at no cost to flavour. It was very similar to all the others lining supermarket shelves. I had absolutely no idea what the scientists were on about. I concluded that they had never eaten a real tomato in their lives. (Like the Canberra food bureaucrats who have never eaten a real piece of cheese.) I won't mention the tomato's name or the lab because they rightly must have failed. In short, tomatoes other than home-grown ones are mostly awful. (Some of the roma variety and dwarf tomatoes at the market are as good as it gets.) Why do we keep buying them? Because better organic alternatives are few and far between and cost more. And, like most fruits and vegetables these days, we have decided that we need tomatoes all year around. Slowish foodies who love the seasonality of all things may pull their heads in.

So grow them, but if, like me, you live in southern Australia, that in itself will be a challenge. We haven't had a good tomato season in years. About one in four is acceptable, one in ten producing bumper crops. But every home-grown tomato is worth the effort of preparing properly a bed of soil, cultivating, fertilizing and pruning your plants as they grow. This isn't a book about gardening, and I'm not even going to outline what I do—and, judging by my performance in recent years, it wouldn't be good advice anyway—but I will say that I always put in at least a couple of plants that produce what used to be called 'cherry' tomatoes. Sweet bite is a good version. They never seem to fail. I think I've cultivated just about every full-sized breed of tomato available. All are OK, but it always surprises me how little difference in yield you get by planting expensive F1 breeds. (Without sending out a search party for my genetics notes from the mid-1960s, I seem to remember F1s were the first, strongest and best cross-breeds.) And they're low in flavour. There is also a new black russian variety that looks disgusting—it has the malignant grey-green of wormy fruit.

Grown on the western Andean slopes, the first tomatoes (called 'golden apples') were yellow. Being members of the *Solanaceae* family—like belladonna—they were said by some until fairly recent times to be poisonous, carcinogenic and just plain boring. In *Food*, Waverley Root cites a Colonel Robert Johnson, who ate a raw tomato in public, saving the day in 1840. And, of course, we may also thank the Italians.

When tomatoes grow well, I keep coming back to one sort and only one for my home garden—grosse lisse, the 'fat smooth' variety that perhaps had French origins. Let your tomatoes ripen on the plant. Do everything needed to keep animals and birds away from them. And when you see a particularly luscious, perfect, big, deep-red grosse lisse and the heart gross leaps, stand amid your staked rows of love apples (another ancient name)—just like the Godfather did—let the sun warm your bare neck, pluck the tomato from the vine, brush it quickly with your knuckly old suburban-peasant's hands and attack it there and then.

Some people sprinkle salt on their tomatoes, others sugar. A tomato farmer once told me his favourite recipe for fresh tomato was simply to season slices on brown-bread toast then munch. It was his idea of heaven. With some luck from the weather gods, it can also be yours.

Freshly opened Pacific oyster

I stress *Pacific* oysters as one of your last destinies with the palate simply because they outstrip all others in succulence and size. They're a kind of epic or special-effects oyster compared with indigenous arthouse bivalves of the New South Wales coast. Moreover, the New South Welsh oyster fishery has abused these marvellous molluscs as long as it has been around, ostensibly for health reasons. The great Sydney rock oyster is subject to ungastronomic indignities from start to finish. It's opened; it's rinsed in fresh water; it's irradiated with ultraviolet light; it has the tendon cut that attaches it to its shell, thereby killing it long before it's eaten. Moreover, specimens treated in such a way are called 'fresh'! What a joke! Nothing could be farther from the truth.

Oysters should be consumed only one way, in my rather zealous view. Freshly opened. And I mean freshly! Opened as shortly before consumption as possible. Preferably, oysters should be opened by those who will eat them, cutting out the middleman and delays between opening and consuming. The oyster should be held horizontal so that the precious juices in which it has spent its life are not spilled out of the shell. Plunge in your oyster knife at the hinge. (The jury is actually still out on where to open an oyster, but I've found the hinge to be the best spot.) Flecks of shell should be removed with a finger; not any metallic implement, anyway, that might taint the juice. And, finally, the tendon or 'foot' of the oyster should be cut by the eater with an oyster fork. Eat oyster and juice together—chew and swallow. There is simply nothing better; this is one of the transcendent experiences of gastronomy. Add lemon juice or shallot-vinegar dressing at your peril. You're corrupting the animal and its home. It's like putting 'metal' weatherboard cladding over an old house. And don't cook oysters.

Several restaurants do the right thing by the brilliant bivalves these days, but most still don't. They wash away its home, its environment. By the time it's eaten, the oyster is sad and grieving. The French eat oysters in months with an 'r'. From May to August—roughly summer—the shellfish are fat with eggs, milky and flabby. In Australia, we have never been so finicky, and some of us inexplicably like oysters pregnant and flabby. Winter is the best time to eat Pacifics, especially if they come from very cold Tasmanian waters. They'll be lean, muscly and full of flavour.

Of the ten or so species Aborigines harvested—one grows on the spectacularly wild Cobourg Peninsula north-east of Darwin—only the Sydney rock (*Crassostrea commercialis*) has been farmed to any degree. It's a tasty bivalve, but pretty miserable in size, prone to microbial contamination and usually treated worse than a six-year-old Brit at a boarding school. Hugely farmed Pacific oysters (*Crassostrea gigas*) are offspring of two shipments brought in hessian sacks from Japan by sea in 1947 and 1948. They were strewn in Albany in Western Australia and Tasmania but did well only on the island's coast, where their husbanding for profit began in the early 1970s. For all that, the biggest-flavoured oysters are the flat brown natives (*Ostrea angasi*), which are hard to farm and have been almost fished out. Give them a try … if you can find them.

Other wonderful seafood, as we know, is harvested from Tasmanian waters. Until quite recently, scallops were grown in plastic mesh lantern cages in some of the cleanest, coldest, purest water on the planet. Because they lived their lives suspended in very deep water and not in their natural habitat—sandy seabeds— they could be eaten whole and even raw, though their richness made the latter a real challenge. (Equally sweet and cloying are raw lobes of roe from freshly opened sea urchins.) Economics meant this method of growing scallops had to be discontinued, but very fine Tasmanian scallops are now being dredged in the wild then purged of their gut-grit on land before sale.

Proper chocolate

People who think they're chocoholics aren't. What they're addicted to is fat, in the form of cocoa butter, and sugar. That chocolate is one of the most corrupted of foodstuffs comes as a surprise to many. It's why I don't like most so-called 'chocolates'. They're simply a concocted contrivance—a kind of gastro dumbing-down, if you like—to exploit the pockets and gastronomic innocence of the vast majority of people. Confectioners shouldn't get away with it, but they do because better chocolate (including proper chocolate) is considerably more expensive, and, paradoxically, harder for the uninitiated to eat. It has what I once called 'a wonderful searing astringency'. Real chocolate is very bitter. But it has a unique rich taste that you should experience at least once.

Why is it so different in flavour from mass-marketed chocolate? Well, only about half of the latter—and sometimes even less—is expensive cocoa content (chocolate). What sells as chocolate is mostly sugar, skimmed-milk powder, sometimes powdered cream, and other additives. For people who don't like chocolate or who have tasted the real stuff, mass-produced chocolate is crudely sweet and vomitous.

To make real chocolate you need to buy a chocolate-making machine called a conche, which usually costs tens of thousands of dollars. Then you need to import chocolate's raw materials—cocoa beans and cocoa liquor, which isn't a liquid at all, but solid black blocks or fragments produced from the beans. (Press it and you get cocoa butter and a residue of powdered cocoa.) The makings for fine chocolate can come from as many as eighteen countries. Finally, you have to be a bit of a magician to blend the various ingredients in the conche in the right way to produce acceptable chocolate.

A good chocolate—it will be very dark—is high in acid and usually about seventy to ninety-nine per cent cocoa. Like gangsters and coffee, it should be strong and bitter. I won't cite any proprietary names, but you will find good chocolate if you take the time to look around. Check for a very dark colour, and, more importantly, a high cocoa content. The higher the better.

Japanese rice crackers at a *shinkansen* station

As you can see, this is not a book about processed food. Yet I couldn't resist adding a unique eating experience that involves factories and machines. Once you've robbed your chosen bank (or become its CEO) I want you to fly straight to Japan and queue up between the yellow lines on the platform of a Japanese *shinkansen* (bullet train) station.

But first you'll need some tucker, and all along the station you'll find glassed-in kiosks selling all manner of snacks and packs, lunchboxes of sushi and sashimi, and even sandwiches in expensive-seeming transparent packaging. So purchase a treat or two from here, if you like, but I want you to move out onto the platform as soon as possible. Perhaps with the exclusion of motor cars, you can buy anything from brightly coloured, glass-fronted, fridge-sized dispensers in Japan. And all I want you to do is find your dispenser—which won't be hard—then the few yen in change you will need to buy a packet of disc-shaped, wafer-thin rice crackers. If Japanese toddlers can make these machines work then you can, too. Your package will be transparent, printed with bright letters in many colours. The crackers will probably be wrapped with as many as three layers of cellophanes and plastics of various sorts and thicknesses.

The bullet train you are waiting for will arrive a minute or so before it's due to leave. You might be privileged enough to watch a change of drivers, two men impeccably uniformed who will draw themselves to attention on the platform and salute one another with white-gloved hands. Pop a cracker in your mouth. Marvel at the precision of Japan, the way the cracker—every cracker in the packet, actually—has the same brilliant, adhesive surface in the mouth, a brittleness transcending belief, and a haunting exotic flavour that might come from land or sea—or even chemicals.

Watch your stationmasters, who will usher you onto the train in the strict lines in which you have queued. Pop another cracker. Through the window, keep one eye on the stationmasters and another on the second hands of the clocks along the platform. At about fifteen seconds to the minute on which your train is due to depart, the stationmasters, standing as straight as goalposts, will turn and raise their arms horizontally first one way along the platform then the other, in unison, white-gloved hands pointing, faces turning with their arms, eyes piercing, expressions solemn. And at precisely, exactly and specifically the sixtieth second of the minute before your train is due to depart you will barely feel a small slide forward. Actually, you will mostly see it; the dispenser on the platform from which you bought your crackers will begin to exit stage left—or right, as the case may be. Within a minute, the train in which you are sitting will be moving quite fast. Only minutes later, it will be travelling like a bullet. Marvel at Japan. Pop another cracker.

Minutes-old sashimi carved from your own catch

Of all the counsel in this book, that which is contained in this article you should consider to be slightly dubious. (And that doesn't mean the other articles are wholly dubious.) There is just so much to the Japanese way with raw fish—its art, precision and history—that the right-thinking gastronome would be wise to consider carefully how to prepare sashimi.

What I'm talking about, you see, is rough and ready—quite prehistoric, really. But it is a gastro-treat. I want you to eat raw fish that is only minutes, if not seconds, out of the water. Preferably, you should have caught the catch yourself. I recommend this particular taste treat because I've experienced it myself in a small and decrepit boat pitching on the chop of the Timor Sea. A group of us was out from Darwin for a couple of days, and among our number was a chef who had brought wasabi paste (Japanese green horseradish) and soy sauce. We cooked fish on our first evening at sea, but after reeling in a bumper catch next morning, we decided to have a sashimi brunch. Finfish species are numerous in the seas to our tropical north, and we had boated such varieties as coral trout and cod, giant trevally, small tuna, red emperor and snapper of several sorts. And with a sharp knife, our chef literally butchered a few of these of different sorts and plated— fairly untidily—a range of misshapen sashimi that had retained the sea's warm temperature. He got out his wasabi paste and soy sauce and we were off.

His long blade glinting, a sashimi chef once told me that the flavour of the fish he presented was affected by how he sliced it. Qualifying to become a sashimi master took years of training, he said, and without the knowledge you couldn't hope to make people weep over your raw-fish slices. And I thought of him as we put down our rods and tucked into our sashimi platter. The flavours were round and full, the mouthfuls filling and nicely chewy. But they somehow lacked the scintillating brilliance of the clean-edged lozenges of cold tuna or salmon that you are served in great sashimi restaurants. For no known scientific reason, the sashimi chef who told me about the importance of precision cutting was, of course, correct. (He even made the point that he could ruin the fish bits if he failed to run his knife through them in a single smooth slash each time.)

It's not generally known that basic sushi—raw fish with vinegared rice and wasabi—has completely different origins from sashimi. Indeed, thin slices of fresh fillet accompany sake as a prelude to a meal at a sushi house—sashimi is a pre-dinner snack. Sushi, on the other hand, originated not because the Japanese *wanted* to eat raw fish but because they needed to preserve their catch. The Chinese had been conserving salted fish in rice since the second century; some South-East Asian tribes had been doing it for even longer. A good idea, the Japanese followed suit, some 500 years after the Chinese.

The process is simple enough, but the Japanese modified it slightly, pressing their salted fish in rice under a stone, keeping it there for anything up to three years. How this idea came about is anyone's guess, but I suspect the pressing was supposed to accelerate the curing. Whenever fish were removed to eat, the rice around them was discarded. By the fifteenth century, fermentation times were drastically shortened to about a month, and not only the fish but the rice was eaten as well.

Dosing the rice with vinegar further strengthened the gastronomic link between the fermented fish and its preserving medium (rice). It also lowered curing times. And by the seventeenth century, salted fish were weighted with a stone over balls of vinegared rice, the curing period being overnight or no more than a day, which amounted to the birth of modern sushi. At the beginning of the nineteenth century, hands began to replace stone weights, and the notion of preservation was dropped altogether. The freshest raw fish were used.

What intrigues me is why the Japanese over centuries replaced a method of preservation with a fresher, rawer gastronomic appreciation of fish. Inscrutable, it is. Perhaps an increasing population and a smaller catch per head (at least until floating fish-factories arrived) meant that there were fewer fish to preserve. But I like to think simple palate appreciation propelled the dietary change.

Caviar

A friend of mine once managed a remote terminus of an Asian airline. Traffic to and from it was relatively light, but the airline kept up appearances, of course, configuring each jet into the customary classes of first, business and desperate. Even though fewer than half-a-dozen superior passengers ever arrived weekly at my friend's very own heart of darkness, the galley in the 747's nose was rigorously stocked with the habitual packed lunch of the rich and famous—champagne and caviar. Purveyed in small jars by a reputable Iranian firm, the caviar was fine

Caspian Sea beluga; the best money could buy. The champagne was Dom. And my friend just pinched it. Almost none of the few passengers ever indulged. Some were religiously inclined, fearing pleasure almost as much as Methodists used to. And these treasures would have been wasted—possibly thrown out beyond their use-by dates in the case of the caviar jars. So he—and eventually his friends—simply helped the airline out, so to speak. I have very fond memories of hearing low hisses, gastro-kisses, emanating from freshly uncapped jars of beluga. We sat back, often with a jar each, a bottle or two of Dom ebbing.

Eat caviar with nothing else. Don't succumb to the nonsense that chopped shallots, minced boiled egg or, heaven forbid, crackers or toast go with these regal fish eggs. Ingredients are pressed on caviar—or, rather, it is pressed on them—to make it go further. Find your own airline, steal your own jars and you shouldn't need to worry about scrimping. And you must use a spoon made of bone, horn or wood to get the caviar out of the jar. Seconds after putting metal into caviar you will notice an unappetizing fishy taste and smell.

Of medium saltiness, caviar—the mostly grey-coloured eggs of several species of the 250-million-year-old dinosaur-age sturgeon—is simply one of the greatest of foods. The ova cling together like frogs' eggs and have a sticky, oily consistency. With a little tongue pressure you smash them, releasing an orgasm of salty, fishy juice.

Beluga is always said to be the best, because of its relatively large size and pale-grey to dark-slate colours. It comes from a fish called *Huso huso,* which also might explain its attraction. The less expensive osetra caviar from *Acipenser gueldenstaedti* is, in my view, a more interesting eat because of its nuttiness and dark-brown to gold colour. Sevruga, the smallest and best-known caviar, is usually black with an oily dark-green tinge and is taken from *Acipenser stellatus.*

Australia used to ban caviar, but it's now back on the shelves. However, its trade and conservation are undermined by gangsters and black marketeers operating where it is fished. Its days are numbered.

Fresh lychee

I wish I'd taken notes. There I was touring the outback of New Caledonia—believe it or not, the main island of New Caledonia has significant scrubby, dry and fairly unattractive wilds—when a photographer and I came upon a tiny village of smallholdings. This place, I soon discovered, nurtured one of life's greatest gastronomic thrills, something so licentious, so libidinously lewd that I felt terrible remorse once I began to eat it. My latent, well and truly lapsed Methodism nudged me remorselessly. Arousing me to what Freud would have called—at least among his women patients—'hysteria' were fresh lychees.

It's no accident that the words 'licentious' and 'lichee' (an alternative spelling) follow one another in my *Macquarie Dictionary*. These fruit are disgustingly beautiful. And so is the tree. Here was a family of local Kanaks, all chocolate smiles and coloured cloths, up skittish ladders and balancing on boxes so that they could rip off great branches of fruit from a very handsome, huge evergreen. Would we like some? Of course, and we bought bagfuls at a ridiculously low price.

Next night, a memorable moment followed when I shared my horde with a gorgeous young woman from Sydney—she'd won a beauty contest and her prize was a trip for two to New Caledonia. Her companion was an equally compelling female friend. We dribbled lychees down our chins for the best part of two hours, gorging strongly, the girls gorgeous. And the more we ate the fruitier became our chat. In the end, I had to send these wonderful women away, you understand. Precaution is everything.

If you haven't had a fresh lychee (*Licthi chinensis*) I'm going to be in all sorts of strife trying to tell you what it's like. They're spherical, about three-quarters the size of a squash ball, and their skin is brown, rough, and brittle. Lychees have to be eaten fresh, because it's only then that the skin is so brittle it virtually shatters like porcelain, and the gelatinous, translucent white fruit inside is brimming with the maximum amount of juice. There is a single pip, which you spit out before breaking into your next lychee. I recently ate at twenty-six Hong Kong restaurants in ten days. My breakfasts were only and always fresh lychees in my hotel room. Some people use them in cooking. It's pointless. If you like filthy food, eat lychees as nature intended.

Raw-milk cheeses

Comparing a great French raw-milk cheese with Australia's best efforts in curdling milk is like trying to find similarities between Bach's music and the doof-doof emanating from a hoon's sedan. In short, there is *no comparison*. Don't let anyone ever get away with telling you Australia's cheeses are fine, good, or of world-champion quality. They're not. Apart from a few fresh examples that are usually only days old and produced from goat's milk, they're terrible. They might look something like real cheese, but they have almost no flavour alongside the best cheeses, and nowhere near the complexities of taste that are built in when milk fresh from the animal is used. (Australia also suffers from a lack of variation in the combinations of soil, climate, animal breeds and feed that go to make the diversity and quality of the best European cheeses.) In accordance with a ridiculous law, Australian cheesemakers must pasteurize their milk before making cheese. Consequently, their efforts are very ordinary. (They claim world championships in America! You know, that great gourmet nation that produced McDonald's and Coke. No self-respecting Gallic cheesemaker would enter a competition in Wisconsin, for a start.)

That's why you really must—this is an essential experience, not to be missed—try a plate of great raw-milk cheeses before you pop off. My principal gastronomic reason for visiting France will forever be to eat real cheese. On the plate should be, at the very least, a camembert, a Brie de Meaux, a Pont l'Evêque and a roquefort, and you should enjoy them with plain crusty bread—not fantasy bake-ups in all their varieties or nuts, dried fruits or celery sticks. (I've named four, but there are many sublime raw-milk English and Italian cheeses you should also try.) And to get the most out of them, drink plain tap water between mouthfuls, not strong red wine. You will notice that a great raw-milk cheese takes you to another gastronomic universe where textures are smooth and unctuous and flavours are rich, powerful, complex and speak of the farm from which they come. I'm not talking strong, unpalatable flavours. These are tastes anyone with absolutely the slightest palate appreciation falls in love with immediately. And these cheeses are not smelly. Good cheese isn't.

In Australia we can't even taste almost all—and certainly the greatest— raw-milk cheeses because they are barred. A tiny few people try to overturn these rules. But we are up against complacent politicians, bureaucrats who don't care and obviously guard their sinecures, and a dairy industry dominated by huge capital interests and lazy dairy farmers. Among these people not a single one is a self-respecting gastronome who would like to enrich the lives of ordinary Australians. (I am not exaggerating; to be able to eat raw-milk cheese considerably enriches your life. It's one reason why the French, in the main, don't emigrate.) No, these people know that to make raw-milk cheese in Australia we should have to install the kind of rigour and order and health protocols that are common in French cheesemaking. And this would take time and effort and money. From their point of view, the status quo is far more comfortable and a lot cheaper. And if there are complaints, they can just perpetuate the lie that the cheese they produce is wonderful, knowing that very few of their compatriots have the knowledge to counter their bluster. It's a classic case of Australian greed, smug lethargy and she'll-be-rightism. If Australian firms tried to pass off their products in France they would be ridiculed. (And that goes for the cheese as well.)

Will Studd, these days a cheese importer who labours under restrictions, and Richard Thomas, a cheesemaker, are two men who could change things—who began to change things in the 1980s. But they have been marginalized. In the early days of small-scale Australian cheesemaking, Will helped to set up artisan cheese factories. Richard, a perfectionist, can't practise his craft to the full. Will fought a valiant campaign against Food Safety Australia New Zealand (FSANZ) by attempting to import a batch of real roquefort, which is a favourite throughout the world and is made from unpasteurized sheep's milk. The shipment made it to Australia, but was quarantined for many months in Will's warehouse. In the end, he was directed by law to discard the roquefort at a suburban tip.

And everywhere you look petty health and dairy-industry bureaucrats, who've never conceded the brilliant complexities of real cheese compared with Australian fakes, call the shots. Not only is raw-milk cheese banned, but FSANZ is also looking to extend prohibitions on imported cheeses. The Australian Specialist Cheesemakers Association, which was set up in 1996 to promote raw-milk cheesemaking, has no interest these days in using unpasteurized milk. At base, its members are too lazy and cheap to implement safety measures to minimize bacterial contamination of raw milk. The politics of it all is Byzantine, the vested interests huge. Easy scaremongering about the dangers of pathogens in unpasteurized milk is the lever claimed by those who benefit from the status quo. (They can easily replicate in pasteurized milk, too.) Yet banning raw-milk cheese on safety grounds makes less sense than banning show jumping, motor cars and anaesthetics, which are all much more dangerous. (Indeed, leaving your house today is going to be a far more perilous exercise than eating a whole wheel of raw-milk camembert.)

Meanwhile, those of us who love real cheese and can see the enormous potential of a proper Australian cheese industry miss out. And so does Australia. I urge you next European trip not to miss great raw-milk cheese. Look for the words *lait cru* (pronounced 'lay croo') on the labels or simply say those words to the people behind the dairy counters, in the cheese shops or at the markets. You will be astonished at the lifetime of sublime eating you've missed out on. And the corollary is, don't buy fancy Australian cheese in Australia. They're substandard—and overpriced.

A ripe mango—the fourth half

A woman friend of mine was once young and came from Far North Queensland. A farm girl and former Miss Something-or-other, she could do marvellous things with fencing wire. And bathers. One grey cold night in London several decades ago, apropos of nothing, she said she was missing mangoes. She was never short of a swimsuit when they were in season, she continued. It was a pity on a hot sunny day not to have a bit of a sunbake as well as a swim. (Girls *wore* their swimmers when they lay on the beach in those days.)

Ripe mangoes plopped everywhere in FNQ, she said, settling back into her narrative—and her beanbag—like a young female Marlow. She'd pick up a couple, halve them carefully, eat the fruit, then fashion a bikini top and bottom from three of the half-skins and a length or three of fencing wire. These cozzies weren't for swimming in, she said across the top of her Foster's can, her brown eyes sparkling, her mini-skirt displaying legs, thighs and powder-blue knickers. But when girls of style emerged naked from the turquoise sea they put on their mango bikinis to have a quick lay around. My mind sped to a quick lay around, but I wrestled it back onto mangoes ... Trying not to think of their shape, of course.

What did you do with the fourth half? I asked innocently. A two-bar radiator blazed uselessly and we both knew we had no more coins. But, as if she had all the time in the world, she began a shocking narrative, and the room temperature rose all by itself ...

To die for

Mangoes with nothing. Just peeled and eaten. A ripe mango. Is there anything more exquisite than that? Probably not. Certainly not that I can think of within its category.

I had been eating mangoes for many years before I was taught the clever method of getting at them without indulging in the slippery business of peeling them. You bisect them longitudinally, cutting as close to the flat ovoid seed as possible. Then you crosshatch the flesh and press each of the two halves inside out. The fruit pops up in handy cubes that are easily detached from the back of the skin.

Who'd have thought, by the way, that there was a type of mango called Kensington Pride. A new inner-city mews development perhaps. But a mango? Apparently, it's a ripper, and with a little luck you might find it at your favourite market stall. But some other mango varieties are even stranger. One is called strawberry (yes strawberry, 'strawberry mango' not being a fruit cocktail), and another is called bullock's heart. Then there is R2E2, which does not glide about the lino and talk funny.

But back to what my friend told me. She had sex with mangoes. And the only thing none of the names above suggests is just what awfully, disgustingly licentious sexual partners mangoes can be. After years of eating them, stripping them of their leathery gear (sorry, I mean skin), and doing amazing things with my tongue all over their slimy bodies (sorry, I'll rephrase that—on second thoughts, I won't), I'm still amazed that they fail to figure in tabletop dancing and Internet porn. (Naturally, my acquaintance with these things is limited.)

Eat them at will, of course, but I think—actually I know, courtesy of my friend—that mangoes could be stars of self-abuse at sex fairs. Indeed, they are a more useful device for women than men. Getting enough grip was the problem, my friend told me that cold London night. I was going to stammer something about making a handle with fencing wire but thought better of it.

Charcuterie

On our honeymoon touring Corsica many years ago, Dominique and I made the painful mistake of over-indulging in charcuterie—the generic name for hams and salamis and other products cured and fermented from the pig. My new wife and her new husband had stopped for lunch in a tiny village in the high rugged hills in the middle of the island. It was April, well before any tourists arrived—those who used to, of course, at a time when Corsica was a lot less popular and more criminal. We were the café's only guests, and we literally said to the *patron*, 'Feed us!' And he did.

A thick oaken platter was produced. On it were slices of several sorts of salamis; two pâtés, one in chunky peasant style; and the meat of three legs of ham from three different pigs (one wild, as I recall) cured for different periods. Corsican salamis and ham are well known for their rich, bucolic flavours, said to come from the island's robust, tough, and very aromatic indigenous herbs—especially a variety of mint—collectively called *maquis*. We were being told the names of the delights we were consuming—*lonzu, coppa* and *prizutto*—but before the *patron* could finish I was into them, gorging on their bushy, salty, fatty, porky richness. Accompanying the charcuterie was rustic, crustic bread and local unsalted butter.

We were left alone to our gastronomic idyll for about half an hour before we began to think that the enormous platter of charcuterie probably constituted the whole meal. So we gorged some more, my frailty in the face of such temptation greater than my wife Dominique's.

But not long after, a sputtering frying pan the size of a dustbin lid was brought to the table. In it were trout, said the *patron*, which were tickled by local boys that morning from the stream in the valley below the village. I was speechless. Varying from the size of big sardines to dinner-plate width, twenty-six fish simply fried in butter awaited. With lemon wedges, salt and pepper, we ate the lot.

To die for

My memory of the main course is indistinct. I feel, looking back, that it must have been the roasted loin of some local animal, possibly a goat that had roamed widely, eating *maquis* as it went. And there must have been wonderful raw-milk cheeses to follow.

I do, though, remember the dessert, because we were asked if we had room for it. Banana fritters, said the *patron*. We would try them, we said weakly. A pile of fresh-fried fritters coated in fine sugar appeared, perhaps a few kilos of them. We could nibble at only one each, and a plastic bag full of them was pressed on us to take away. I could barely walk, scarcely making it to our hire car. But six hours later I was ready to eat again, such are the digestive capacities of youth. And I began with charcuterie.

Corsican charcuterie was not the first I had eaten; I had engulfed terrines and pâtés since living in France. But part of the mystery and reverence the French hold for pig products inhered in my brother-in-law Pierre's once whispering in awe that we were about to eat 'pâté en croûte'—pâté in a crust. It was great and I loved it, but it was nothing more than what we might call a classy sausage roll.

Charcuterie is terribly forgiving, and excellent salamis and hams are made ubiquitously by big manufacturers and backyard hobbyists. I find more quality variation in hams than salamis. Be choosy. And I must say that the best prosciutto I've eaten was made by Steve of Bundoora, my middle son's father-in-law, in his backyard. Perhaps it's the air in the northern suburbs of Melbourne, but his salamis and hams cure under the eaves in a meat safe. They are sublime. He finds them a lot of trouble to make and, if you're not careful, you can lose a leg of ham at considerable cost, even if you club together with relatives—as Steve does—to buy and kill the pig.

And for a transcendental treat, you should try the Serrano ham of Spain (*see* 'Museo del Jamón').

Lady in pink

You can buy them still, apparently, but it's quite a search. Snow apples were the most memorable fruit of my childhood. And it wasn't so much because they were particularly sweet or had full flavour. It was the blinding whiteness of their flesh when you bit into them. In the shelter-sheds of Australia and under its peppercorn trees, a nation's children squinted from apple-blindness. (Children never had sunglasses then.) There were other varieties of apple—gravensteins and rome beauties and cox's orange pippins—but there was no more sensational eat than a snow apple. No bigger boast could be extracted from a brownpaper lunchbag.

Only one variety of apple has impressed me as much. Moreover, it's a fairly recently marketed variety. It's called Pink Lady. Strictly speaking, that name should be followed by a registered trademark, because the name is owned by Apple and Pear Australia Limited and it's conquering the world. Pink Ladies are a brilliant apple not only because they are extremely tasty. They also provide an exemplary balance of sweetness and tartness. Consumers have gone rapturous about them; they're tangy, aromatic and even 'effervescent', said someone. They're a brand of apple with its very own website. (On which, by the way, it's said that Pink Lady apples mean 'fun, fitness and flirtation'.) And Pink Ladies even sponsored a four-man attempt on the world record for crossing the Atlantic west to east by rowboat. (Unfortunately, the boat broke up a few hundred kilometres from the finish.)

And while Australian exports of Pink Lady apples are growing steeply, other countries—principally the United States, Chile and South Africa—are getting into the act. Pink Lady, you see, is only a marketing name, and anyone can buy a tree producing cripps pink apples, which are precisely the same thing. Australia merely owns the Pink Lady name, which applies to cripps pink apples graded under certain criteria to be of the highest quality. (They must, for instance, have the remarkable Pink Lady blush over at least forty per cent of their area.) Cripps pink itself is all-Australian, an apple bred in 1973 at the Stoneville Research Station in Western Australia by John Cripps from a cross between golden delicious and lady williams.

The future for Pink Ladies is huge. Australia will continue to gain from their royalties, but you can be sure that most of the global income from the apple itself, and cripps pink fruit, has got away.

Raw fugu fish

Of the one hundred eating experiences recommended in this book, you should try this one last. For a simple reason: fugu fish—especially their inner organs—can kill. Yet year in, year out, thousands of Japanese gourmets gamble their lives with an ugly, snub-nosed finfish that inflates when aroused. Fugu are one of many related species worldwide that are variously known as pufferfish, blowfish or porcupine fish (because the skin of the latter bristles with needles). You will have seen relatives of Japan's legendary fugu, ballooned and dead, on beaches around Australia. And I recall that common rockpool 'toadies', which resemble fugu in shape but are much smaller, were said to be poisonous and therefore inedible.

Fugu require extra-careful preparation in specialist restaurants because they contain a nerve poison, tetrodoxin, that can kill in even the most minute quantities. (A big fugu contains enough poison to kill around thirty humans, I've read.) In fugu, the poison concentrates in the liver and other internal organs, which are prohibited from sale. Paper-thin slices of fugu flesh, though, are plated for extravagant sums. Apparently they have a bland taste, chewy texture and can numb the lips nicely.

I say 'apparently', of course, because I haven't tasted fugu and probably won't. You'll one-up me comprehensively if you do. I don't think I'd ever chance my life with a fish because I've done it once already. Inadvertently, of course.

Another restaurant reviewer asked me to accompany him some years ago to a French restaurant in Melbourne. For main course, I chose what was billed as 'yellowfin tuna' steak with an accompanying 'champagne' sauce. When it arrived, the cross-section of fish was relatively thin and of good size. The flesh was white, apart from dark muscle around the vertebral column. A minute or so after trying some dark meat near the bone I noticed my lips tingling. Not wanting to make a fuss, I mentioned it only in passing to my colleague and ate some more. He thought the tingling sensation might have come from the 'champagne' in the sauce!

Within minutes, I felt hot and sweaty and became flushed. I had trouble catching my breath, and my heart rate accelerated. My lips were no longer tingling; they were numb. Indeed, my lower jaw was fast approximating the feeling you get after a deep anaesthetic jab at the dentist's. I asked my colleague if I looked red. Not just red, he replied, but scarlet. And I was expanding— pufferfish style, you might say—to several times my usual size.

We dashed back to the newspaper for which we both worked and I spent the afternoon in the sick bay. At intervals, I took four pills prescribed to counter ciguatera poison, which is picked up at certain times of the year by pelagic fishes—often from the tuna and mackerel families—that graze on coral. If you're unlucky, these big sea-grazers will pass ciguatera on. Captain Cook lost men because they ingested ciguatera in mackerel. My eyes became slits, every square centimetre of my skin was crimson and I panted and puffed all afternoon with a heart rate of around 200. I was sent home by taxi several hours later and took more than a week to recover.

Let me know what fugu is like.

To die for

ACKNOWLEDGEMENTS

My thanks must first go to my agent Margaret Gee, who had the idea for this book. Then my gratitude goes to the entire team at Murdoch Books, led by chief executive Juliet Rogers, who literally pounced on it. They knew almost nothing about me, yet trusted me to write whatever I liked in the shape that best suited me. Finally, I must also thank Anouska Jones, who worked under extremely tight deadlines to hone my words.

BIBLIOGRAPHY

Bocuse, Paul, *Le Gibier*, Flammarion, Paris, 1973

Brunning, Leslie H., *The Australian Gardener*, Robertson & Mullens Ltd,
     Melbourne, 1942

Closs, Amanda, *Tastes of the Channel Isles*, Ampersand Press, 1983

Dannini, Tiberio, *Pasta*, Thomas Nelson, Melbourne, 1984

Downes, Stephen, *Advanced Australian Fare*, Allen & Unwin, Sydney, 2002

Fulton, Margaret, *Encyclopedia of Food & Cookery*, Octopus Books, Sydney, 1984

Green and Gold Cookery Book, Combined Congregational and Baptist Churches of
     South Australia, Adelaide, c. 1940

Hopkins, Jerry, *Strange Foods*, Periplus, Hong Kong, 1999

Larousse Gastronomique, Hamlyn, London, 1976

Michel, Albin, *Les Recettes Secrètes des Meilleurs Restaurants de France*, Albin
     Michel, Paris, 1972

Root, Waverley, *Food*, Simon & Schuster, New York, 1980

Simpson, Ken & Day, Nicolas, *The Birds of Australia*, Lloyd O'Neil, Melbourne, 1984

Symons, Michael, *One Continuous Picnic*, Duck Press, Adelaide, 1982

INDEX

Published in 2005 by Murdoch Books Pty Limited

Murdoch Books Pty Limited Australia
Pier 8/9, 23 Hickson Road, Millers Point NSW 2000
Phone : 61 (0) 2 8220 2000 Fax : 61 (0) 2 8220 2558

Murdoch Books UK Limited
Erico House, 6th Floor North, 93/99 Upper Richmond Road,
Putney, London SW15 2TG
Phone : 44 (0) 20 8785 5995   Fax : 44 (0) 20 8785 5985

Chief Executive: Juliet Rogers
Publisher: Kay Scarlett
Editorial Director: Diana Hill
Design concept and designer: Vivien Valk
Project manager: Paul McNally
Editor: Anouska Jones
Production: Monika Paratore

National Library of Australia Cataloguing-in-Publication Data: Downes, Stephen (Stephen L.).
To die for : 100 gastronomic experiences to have before you die. Bibliography. Includes index.
ISBN 1 74045 591 6. 1. Food—Miscellanea. 2. Gastronomy—Miscellanea.
3. Restaurants—Australia—Miscellanea. I. Title.

Printed in Australia by Griffin Press
Copyright © Murdoch Books 2005
Text copyright © Stephen Downes 2005
Cover photography by Steven Murray

Please note, the following terms have been used throughout *To Die For*
(international alternatives are given in parentheses):
capsicum (pepper)
caster (superfine) sugar
coriander (cilantro)
eggplant (aubergine)
prawns (shrimp)
rocket (arugula)